Coaching Math Workshop

Coaching math workshops? This invaluable resource from beloved guru Dr. Nicki Newton has everything you need to help your teachers and students be successful! Dr. Nicki saves you time and prep work by providing a plethora of tools to help you with each step. She provides an overview of the workshop; getting to know you activities; forms for goal setting, reflections, PD planning, and feedback; calendars; to do lists; data and material logs; lists of things to buy; planning sheets for book studies; and more! With this book's handy checklists and tools, you'll have everything you need to coach math workshop at your fingertips!

Dr. Nicki Newton has been an educator for over 30 years, working both nationally and internationally with students of all ages. She has worked on developing Math Workshop and Guided Math Institutes around the country; visit her website at www.drnickinewton.com. She is also an avid blogger (www.guidedmath.wordpress.com), tweeter (@drnickimath) and pinner (www.pinterest.com/drnicki7).

T0383793

Also Available from Dr. Nicki Newton

(www.routledge.com/eyeoneducation)

Guided Math Lessons in Kindergarten:
Getting Started

Guided Math Lessons in First Grade:
Getting Started

Guided Math Lessons in Second Grade:
Getting Started

Guided Math Lessons in Third Grade:
Getting Started

Guided Math Lessons in Fourth Grade:
Getting Started

Guided Math Lessons in Fifth Grade:
Getting Started

Day-by-Day Math Thinking Routines
in Kindergarten:
40 Weeks of Quick Prompts and Activities

Day-by-Day Math Thinking Routines
in First Grade:
40 Weeks of Quick Prompts and Activities

Day-by-Day Math Thinking Routines
in Second Grade:
40 Weeks of Quick Prompts and Activities

Day-by-Day Math Thinking Routines
in Third Grade:
40 Weeks of Quick Prompts and Activities

Day-by-Day Math Thinking Routines
in Fourth Grade:
40 Weeks of Quick Prompts and Activities

Day-by-Day Math Thinking Routines
in Fifth Grade:
40 Weeks of Quick Prompts and Activities

Leveling Math Workstations in Grades K–2:
Strategies for Differentiated Practice

Daily Math Thinking Routines in Action:
Distributed Practices Across the Year

Mathematizing Your School:
Creating a Culture for Math Success
Co-authored by Janet Nuzzie

Math Problem Solving in Action:
Getting Students to Love Word Problems,
Grades K-2

Math Problem Solving in Action:
Getting Students to Love Word Problems,
Grades 3-5

Fluency Doesn't Just Happen with Addition
and Subtraction:
Strategies and Models for Teaching
the Basic Facts
With Alison Mello and Ann Elise Record

Math Workshop in Action:
Strategies for Grades K-5

Math Running Records in Action:
A Framework for Assessing Basic Fact
Fluency in Grades K-5

Math Workstations in Action:
Powerful Possibilities for Engaged Learning
in Grades 3-5

Coaching Math Workshop

A Must-Have Collection of Planning Forms, Checklists, Reflection Sheets, Observation Logs and More that Puts Everything You Need to Coach Math Workshop at Your Fingertips!

Dr. Nicki Newton

Routledge
Taylor & Francis Group

NEW YORK AND LONDON

Designed cover image: © Shutterstock
Cover concept by Gabrielle Alilio

First published 2024
by Routledge
605 Third Avenue, New York, NY 10158

and by Routledge
4 Park Square, Milton Park, Abingdon, Oxon, OX14 4RN

Routledge is an imprint of the Taylor & Francis Group, an informa business

© 2024 Newton Education Solutions

ISBN: 978-1-032-56373-2 (pbk)
ISBN: 978-1-003-45897-5 (ebk)

DOI: 10.4324/9781003458975

Typeset in Degular
by KnowledgeWorks Global Ltd.

Many of the resources in this book are also available as free downloads so you can print them for your own use. To access these resources, please go to https://resourcecentre.routledge.com/

About the Author

Dr. Nicki Newton has been an educator for 30 years, working both nationally and internationally, with students of all ages. Having spent the first part of her career as a literacy and social studies specialist, she built on those frameworks to inform her math work. She believes that math is intricately intertwined with reading, writing, listening, and speaking. She has worked on developing Math Workshop and Guided Math Institutes around the country. Most recently, she has been helping districts and schools nationwide to integrate their State Standards for Mathematics and think deeply about how to teach these within a Math Workshop Model. Dr. Nicki works with teachers, coaches, and administrators to make math come alive by considering the powerful impact of building a community of mathematicians who make meaning of real math together. When students do real math, they learn it. They own it, they understand it, and they can do it. Every one of them. Dr. Nicki is also an avid blogger (www.guidedmath.wordpress.com) and Pinterest pinner (www.pinterest.com/drnicki7/).

Table of Contents

Table of Contents

Table of Contents

Table of Contents

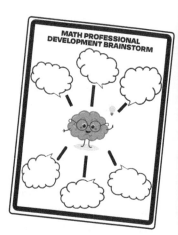

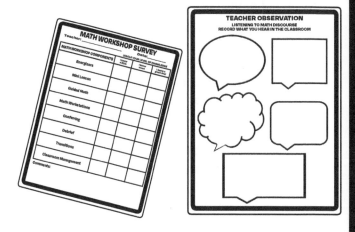

An Introduction to Math Workshop

 DOI: 10.4324/9781003458975-1

Math Workshop is an approach to teaching mathematics. There are 3 Parts to a Math Workshop: 1) The Introduction 2) The Student Activity Period 3) The Debrief.

Math Workshop in Action

The Introduction

- Energizers/Routines
- Problem Solving
- Mini-Lesson

The Student Activity Period

- Guided Math
- Math Workstations
- Conferring

The Debrief

- Whole Class Discussion
- Exit Slips
- Reflections

Math Workshop in Action

There are many different ways to do a Math Workshop. The ideal way is to do Math Workshop every day, with all of the components. Some teachers do the whole workshop, but only 2-3 times a week. Some teachers do some elements every day. For example, they might do the Introduction and the Debrief on some days. They will use other days to do the Student Activity Period.

In this book you will find all the forms you need to coach the different sections of Math Workshop. There are forms that take a look at the entire workshop and there are forms that take a deep dive into the individual elements of workshop. This book is made for coaches who coach Math Workshop!

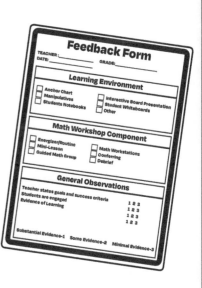

Math Workshop in Action

As we coach Math Workshop, we are thinking about the 6 essential elements: Data-Driven, Differentiation, Standards-Based, Rigorous, Scaffolded and Engaging.

6 Essential Elements

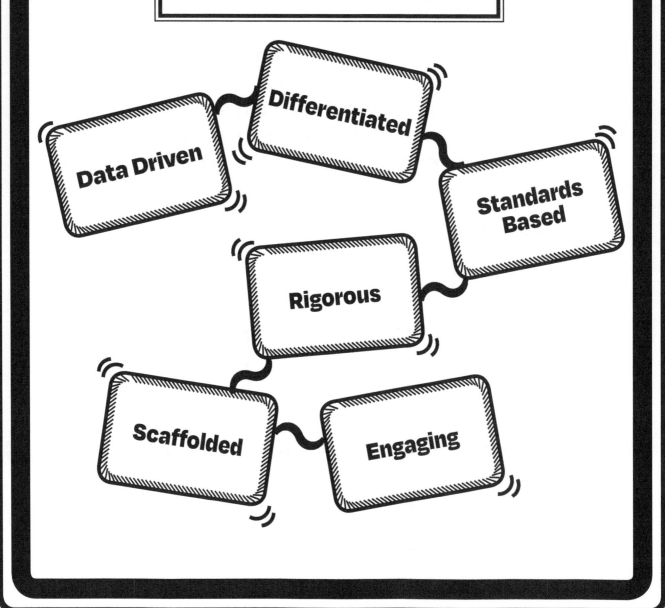

As you coach Math Workshop you will want to keep these elements in mind. You will need to work with teachers on different types of assessment and how we use it to inform and drive instruction. You will want to consider the ways in which teachers are using the data to differentiate instruction. You will want to think about helping the teachers to unpack the standards in ways that are accessible to students. Students should know what they are doing, why they are doing it and what it looks like when they can do it. You will want to help teachers to think about the levels of rigor that they are using in their mini-lesson, guided math lessons and math workstations. Coaches can also help teachers figure out ways to scaffold access for all learners. Finally, you will want to work with teachers on weaving engagement throughout their lessons!

Great Math Workshops only happen when management is in place. As the saying goes, "Classroom Management happens way before the classroom gets there." Coaches oftentimes have to help teachers with classroom management. In this book you will find various tools to observe classroom management and help teachers think through any issues that they may be having.

Throughout the book, you will see many different templates and tools that specifically address different parts of Math Workshop. Coaches help teachers plan informative mini-lessons, effective small group instruction and productive workstations. Coaches help teachers think through if menus or rotations are best for their classroom situation. Coaches help teachers to plan both the opening and closing of Math Workshop.

QUOTES

The difference between ordinary and extraordinary is that little extra.

— Jimmy Johnson

A coach is someone who can give correction without causing resentment.

— John Wooden

My responsibility is leadership, and the minute I get negative, that is going to have an influence on my team.

— Don Shula

How do you coach into the extraordinary? What does it take to get everybody to reach their fullest potential? What is your role as a coach in this?

How do you do this? There is both an art and a science to helping people help themselves. Does your feedback actually "feed forward?" Does it motivate? Does it encourage?

What do you do to stay positive? What are your routines for centering yourself? What do you do when you are feeling frustrated? How do you keep that feeling from spilling out?

QUOTES

The Coaching Habit:
Say Less, Ask More

- Bungay-Stanier

What does this mean to you? How does it apply to your daily coaching practice? How could you get better at this skill? Why do you think this is important?

Introduction

The purpose of this book is to help Math Coaches to coach Math Workshop. Here you will find all the tools you need, organized into a system to help you get the job done. The purpose of this book is to have all of the essential forms together in one place. Each of these forms are available in printed form in this book and many are also available in customizable versions in the companion to the book (https://resourcecentre.routledge.com/).

Math Coaches are very busy. There is so much to do. Where to start? What to do first? How do I get to know my teachers? How do I improve my own pedagogy? How do I start the challenging conversations? How do I start any of the conversations? What do I say? How do I say it? How do I encourage, support, gently push forward initiatives that are great for students and negotiate the multiple relationships that come with coaching?

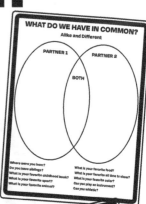

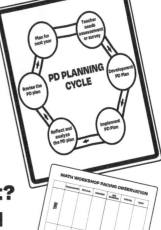

In this book you will find tools and resources to help you answer these questions.

You will find different ways to approach situations. Different approaches to talking about teaching practice. Many ways to capture what you see, hear and feel when you go into classrooms to support teachers!

There are 14 sections in this book to help you on your math coaching journey!

GETTING TO KNOW YOU

These forms help you get to know the teachers you will be working with during the school year. Who they are, what they like, how they want to experience professional development and more. There are a series of surveys and questionnaires that will help coaches to better understand the teachers.

INITIATIVES

These forms help outline the district and school initiatives so that they are the velcro to which your coaching sticks.

PROFESSIONAL DEVELOPMENT PLANNING PAGES

These forms are like a PD planning toolkit. You will find PD planners, PD surveys, PD exit slips, PD brainstorming sheets and more.

COACHING MATH WORKSHOP

These forms help structure general and specific observations in Math Workshop. There are various forms for observing different parts of Math Workshop including energizers/routines, mini-lessons, guided math groups, math workstations, conferences and the debrief. They help coaches to catch what is said and done and keep them on a record so that they can effectively debrief with specific data points and plan for next steps.

INSTRUCTIONAL SUPPORT LOGS

These support logs capture where you were throughout the day and what you did. There are different formats, where you can capture your work with individual teachers or groups of teachers.

COACHING THE PLANNING OF MATH WORKSHOP

These forms help the coach ask the right questions when planning the different components of Math Workshop.

COACHING REFLECTIONS

These forms help coaches reflect on their journey. They help coaches think about their goals, their accomplishments and spaces and places that they need to grow.

GOAL SETTING WITH TEACHERS

These forms help guide goal setting with teachers about Math Workshop. Where are they on the Math Workshop journey? What are their strengths? Where do they need to do better? How will they plot out that path? What help do they need?

COACHING DATA
These forms facilitate data conversations. What does the data tell us about studet learning? What do we do with that information?

CALENDARS
These yearly, quarterly, monthly, weekly and daily planning calendars help coaches schedule their time.

TO DO LISTS
These lists help coaches stay organized and prioritize their tasks.

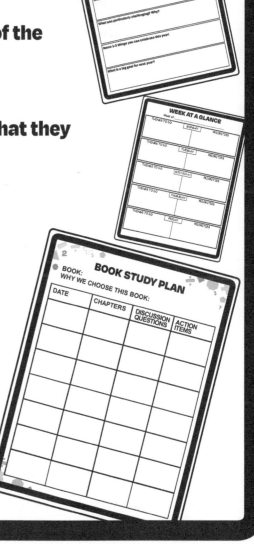

MATERIALS LOG
These forms help coaches keep track of the materials that they loan out to others.

THINGS TO BUY
These sheets help coaches organize what they need to buy and why.

BOOK STUDY PLANNING SHEETS
These sheets help coaches plan book studies.

Getting to Know You

DOI: 10.4324/9781003458975-2

What You will Find in this Section!

In this section you will find forms to start the year. There are surveys, questionnaires, ice breakers and more! There are forms that you can use to meet and greet the staff. There is a Find Someone Who Game as well as an Energizer. There is also a Beginning of the Year Survey to give to teachers at the beginning of the year so that you can begin to get to know who they are and what type of PD they would like. There is also a Coaching menu to help teachers understand the types of support that you can do for them. (During the first month of school, it is great to try and set up a 1 to 1 conference with each teacher so that you can set individual teacher goals for the year.)

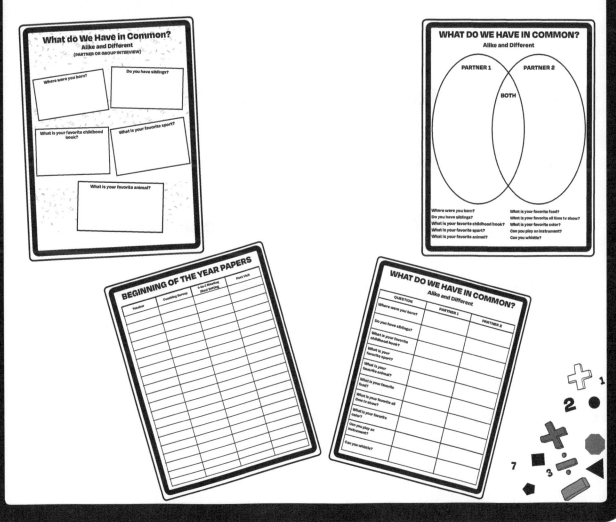

Getting to Know You.....

1. What makes you smile?

2. What do you want to learn about Math Workshop this year?

3. What are your professional goals for this year?

4. How do you like to learn new things?

Read Professional Text   Watch Video Clips

Take a Digital Course   Attend PD Events

By Yourself   With a Partner   As a Team

5. In what ways would you like the instructional/math coach to support you this year?

TEACHER QUESTIONNAIRE

NAME:_____

DATE: _____

WHO AM I?

WHAT I LIKE PEOPLE TO CALL ME:
_____

BIRTHDAY: _____
FAVORITE SNACK:_____
FAVORITE FOOD: _____
FAVORITE DRINK: _____
FAVORITE COLOR: _____
SOMETHING ABOUT ME YOU'D
NEVER GUESS: _____
_____

WHAT PART OF MATH WORKSHOP DO I NEED HELP WITH?

PLEASE CHECK ALL THAT APPLY:

☐ ENERGIZERS/ROUTINES
☐ MINI-LESSON
☐ GUIDED MATH
☐ MATH WORKSTATIONS
☐ CONFERRING
☐ DEBRIEFING

WHAT KIND OF PD DO I PREFER?

PLEASE CHECK ALL THAT APPLY:

☐ IN-PERSON
☐ ONLINE
☐ TEAM MEETING
☐ ONE-TO-ONE
☐ BEFORE SCHOOL
☐ AFTER SCHOOL
☐ DURING SCHOOL

OTHER THOUGHTS:

??? FIND SOMEONE WHO...

Find someone who loves the color purple.	Find someone who loves math.	Find someone who likes asparagus.	Find someone who was born abroad.	Find someone who speaks another language at home.
Find someone who has been teaching for more than 10 years.	Find someone who has been teaching for 1 to 3 years.	Find someone who went away this summer.	Find someone who has siblings.	Find someone who has a pet.
Find someone who loves math.	Find someone who reads more than 7 books a year.	FREE	Find someone who loves rollercoasters.	Find someone who has ridden on a motorcycle.
Find someone who loves fruit.	Find someone who loves chocolate.	Find someone who has sisters.	Find someone who has brothers.	Find someone who has kids.
Find someone who loves to color.	Find someone who loves to go to the movies.	Find someone who loves to play sports.	Find someone who loves to watch sports.	Find someone who is a vegetarian.

26

What Do We Have in Common?
Alike and Different
(PARTNER OR GROUP INTERVIEW)

Where were you born?

Do you have siblings?

What is your favorite childhood book?

What is your favorite sport?

What is your favorite animal?

What Do We Have in Common?
Alike and Different
(PARTNER OR GROUP INTERVIEW)

What is your favorite food?

What is your favorite all time tv show?

What is your favorite color?

Can you play an instrument?

Can you whistle?

What Do We Have in Common?
Alike and Different
(PARTNER OR GROUP INTERVIEW)

WHAT DO WE HAVE IN COMMON?
Alike and Different

PARTNER 1   PARTNER 2

BOTH

Where were you born?

Do you have siblings?

What is your favorite childhood book?

What is your favorite sport?

What is your favorite animal?

What is your favorite food?

What is your favorite all time tv show?

What is your favorite color?

Can you play an instrument?

Can you whistle?

WHAT DO WE HAVE IN COMMON?

Alike and Different

QUESTION	PARTNER 1	PARTNER 2
Where were you born?		
Do you have siblings?		
What is your favorite childhood book?		
What is your favorite sport?		
What is your favorite animal?		
What is your favorite food?		
What is your favorite all time tv show?		
What is your favorite color?		
Can you play an instrument?		
Can you whistle?		

BEGINNING OF THE YEAR

Teacher	Coaching Survey	1-to-1 Meeting /Goal Setting	First Visit

District/School Initiatives

 DOI: 10.4324/9781003458975-3

What You will Find in this Section!

In this section you will find forms to help you organize everything that has to do with district and school initiatives!

District Math Initiatives

Component of Math Workshop	Initiative	Evidence of Implementation

School Math Initiatives

Component of Math Workshop	Initiative	Evidence of Implementation

PRINCIPAL MEETING NOTES

Date	Notes	Action Items	Follow Up Date

Professional Development Planning Pages

DOI: 10.4324/9781003458975-4

QUOTES

"An hour of planning can save you 10 hours of doing."

Dale Carnegie.

Do you plan? How often? What are your routines around planning for the day, week, month, quarter and year? What is working? What do you need to change?

QUOTES

"A goal without a plan is just a wish."

Antoine de Saint-Exupéry.

How are you at goal setting? Do you set goals with action plans? Do you put dates on those plans? Do you reflect and revise once you have completed those goals?

What You will Find in this Section!

In this section you will find different templates to help you plan and organize professional development PD meetings. There are PD Surveys, PD Brainstorms, PD Sign-In sheets, PD exit slips and more.

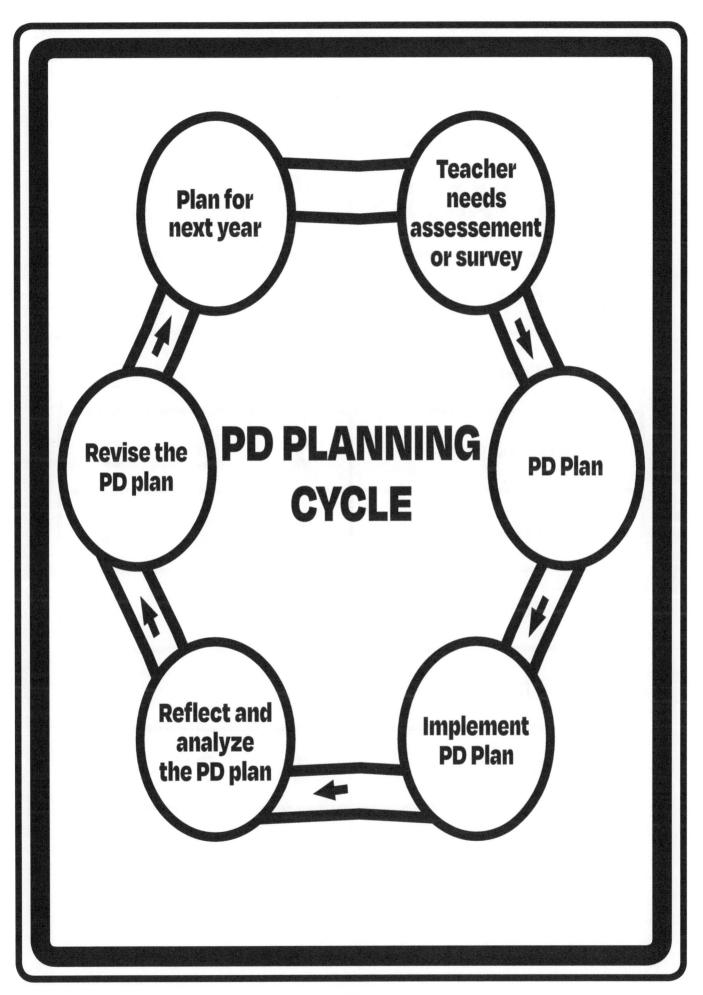

Math Workshop PD Survey

FOCUS AREAS	CIRCLE YOUR LEVEL OF KNOWLEDGE		
Energizers/Routines	1	2	3
Mini-Lesson	1	2	3
Guided Math	1	2	3
Math Workstations	1	2	3
Conferring	1	2	3
Debrief	1	2	3
Transitions	1	2	3
Classroom Management	1	2	3

Key: 1 - little   2 - some   3 - a great deal

Teacher: _____ **Date:** _____

Math Workshop PD Survey

FOCUS AREAS	CIRCLE YOUR LEVEL OF KNOWLEDGE		
Energizers/Routines	1	2	3
Mini-Lesson	1	2	3
Guided Math	1	2	3
Math Workstations	1	2	3
Conferring	1	2	3
Debrief	1	2	3
Transitions	1	2	3
Classroom Management	1	2	3

Key: 1 - little   2 - some   3 - a great deal

Choose your PD Adventure

How do you prefer PD?

☐ Book Study Group

☐ One on One Coaching

☐ Digital Course

☐ Other _____

When do you prefer PD?

☐ Before School

☐ After School

☐ Other _____

MATH WORKSHOP SURVEY

Teacher: _____ **Date:**_____

CIRCLE YOUR LEVEL OF KNOWLEDGE

MATH WORKSHOP COMPONENTS	I know a little.	I know some.	I know a great deal.
Energizers/Routines			
Mini-Lesson			
Guided Math			
Math Workstations			
Conferring			
Debrief			
Transitions			
Classroom Management			

Comments:

MATH PROFESSIONAL DEVELOPMENT BRAINSTORM

DATE:_____ TOPIC:_____

WHAT SHOULD WE DO?

MATH PROFESSIONAL DEVELOPMENT BRAINSTORM

WHAT SHOULD WE DO?	WHY SHOULD WE DO IT?	WHEN SHOULD WE DO IT?

MATH PROFESSIONAL DEVELOPMENT BRAINSTORM

MATH PROFESSIONAL DEVELOPMENT BRAINSTORM

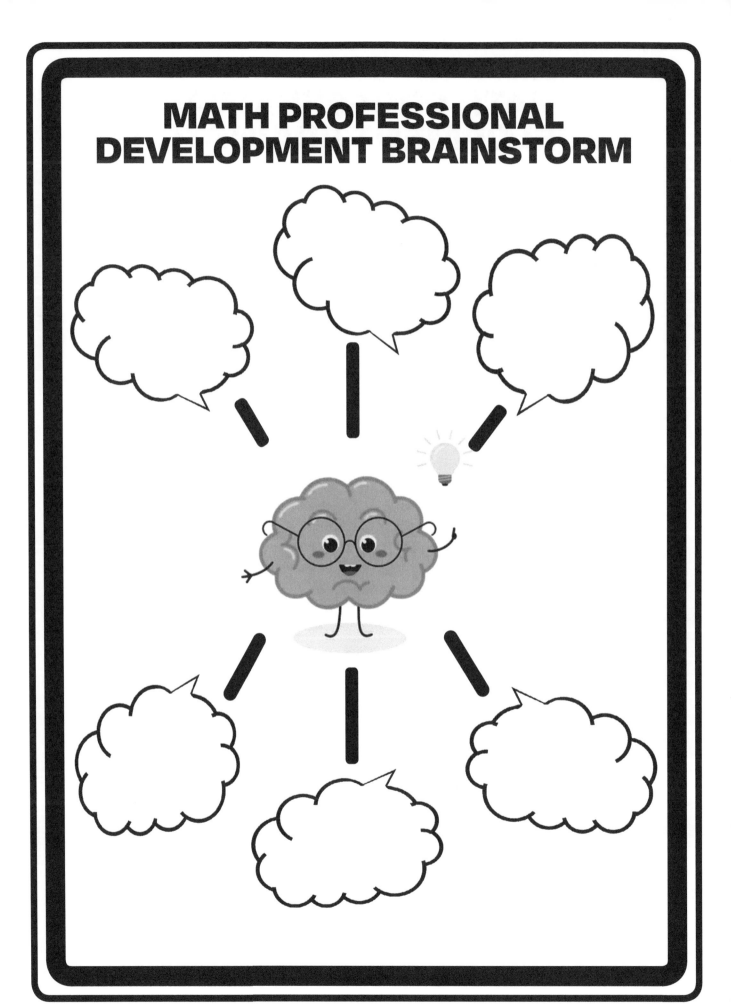

Planning Professional Development

Topic: _____

Date: _____ Time: _____

What are we going to do?	What do we need for it? Materials/Supplies/Tools

Why are we going to do it?	How will we know it was successful?

MATH PROFESSIONAL DEVELOPMENT SIGN-IN

DATE:_____   TOPIC:_____

NAME	SIGNATURE

MATH PROFESSIONAL DEVELOPMENT SIGN-IN

DATE:_____ TOPIC:_____

NAME	SIGNATURE	TIME IN - TIME OUT

MATH PROFESSIONAL DEVELOPMENT SIGN-IN

DATE:_____   TOPIC:_____

NAME	MORNING	AFTERNOON

Grade Level Meeting Notes

Topic: _____   Grade: _____

Date: _____   Time: _____

Priority Items	Things We Are Thinking About

Next Steps	Notes

Grade Level Meeting Notes

Topic:_____   Grade:_____

Date:_____   Time:_____

Priority Items

Things We Are Thinking About

Next Steps

Notes

TEACHER MEETING LOG

NAME: _____   DATE:_____

NOTES

_____
_____
_____
_____
_____
_____
_____
_____
_____

FOLLOW UP DATE: _____   FOLLOW UP DONE ☐

TEACHER MEETING LOG

NAME: _____   DATE:_____

NOTES

FOLLOW UP DATE: _____   FOLLOW UP DONE ☐

PD EXIT SLIP

Name: _____   **Date:** _____

One Take Away

One Question

Next Steps

PD EXIT SLIP

Name: _____   **Date:** _____

One Take Away

One Question

Next Steps

PD EXIT TICKET

Name: _____
Date: _____

What is one big take away?

Other thoughts

PD EXIT TICKET

Name: _____
Date: _____

What is one big take away?

Other thoughts

PD EXIT TICKET

Name: _____
Date: _____

What is one big take away?

Other thoughts

PD EXIT TICKET

Name: _____
Date: _____

What is one big take away?

Other thoughts

QUICK CHAT SLIP

Name: _____   Date:_____

Topic

When can you meet?

Right Now   Recess   Lunch   After School

QUICK CHAT SLIP

Name: _____   Date:_____

Topic

When can you meet?

Right Now   Recess   Lunch   After School

QUICK CHAT SLIP

Name: _____   Date:_____

Topic

When can you meet?

Right Now   Recess   Lunch   After School

QUICK CHAT SLIP

Name: _____   Date:_____

Topic

When can you meet?

Right Now   Recess   Lunch   After School

QUICK CHAT SLIP

Name: _____   Date:_____

Topic

When can you meet?

Right Now   Recess   Lunch   After School

QUICK CHAT SLIP

Name: _____   Date:_____

Topic

When can you meet?

Right Now   Recess   Lunch   After School

QUICK CHAT SLIP

Name: _____   Date: _____

Topic

When can you meet?

Right Now   Recess   Lunch   After School

QUICK CHAT SLIP

Name: _____   Date: _____

Topic

When can you meet?

Right Now   Recess   Lunch   After School

QUICK CHAT SLIP

Name: _____   Date: _____

Topic

When can you meet?

Right Now   Recess   Lunch   After School

QUICK CHAT SLIP

Name: _____   Date: _____

Topic

When can you meet?

Right Now   Recess   Lunch   After School

Math Coaching Menu

Coaching Math in General

Class Visit	Demo/ Model Lesson	Coaching Cycle	Peer Coaching
Co-Teach	Co-Plan	Reviewing Students' Work	Data Chat
Goal Setting	Fostering Engagement	Differentiation	Building Math Vocabulary
Math Picture Books	Assessment Support	Technology in Math Workshop	Building a Math Environment (Anchor Charts, Bulletin Boards, etc)

Math Coaching Menu
Coaching Math in General

Class Visit

Demo/ Model Lesson

Coaching Cycle

Peer Coaching

Co-Teach

Co-Plan

Reviewing Students' Work

Data Chat

Goal Setting

Fostering Engagement

Differentiation

Building Math Vocabulary

Math Picture Books

Assessment Support

Technology in Math Workshop

Building a Math Environment (Anchor Charts, Bulletin Boards, etc)

Math Coaching Menu

Coaching Math Workshop

Planning the Flow of Math Workshop	**Energizers and Routines**
Guided Math	**Math Workstations**
Debrief	**Mini-Lessons**
Conferring	**Classroom Management**

Math Coaching Menu
Coaching Math Workshop

- Planning the Flow of Math Workshop
- Energizers and Routines
- Guided Math
- Math Workstations
- Debrief
- Mini-Lessons
- Conferring
- Classroom Management

Coaching Math Workshop

DOI: 10.4324/9781003458975-5

> "If you want to build a ship, don't drum up people to collect wood and don't assign them tasks and work, but rather teach them to long for the endless immensity of the sea."
> **Little Prince**

How do you get buy-in?

How do you build efforts from the ground up?

How do you get everybody as excited as you are?

Why is that important?

How is it different when teachers feel like they are part of making the plan?

What You will Find in this Section!

In this section you will find many different types of tools, checklists, rubrics and more for observing and coaching Math Workshop. These helpful templates allow you to zero in on specific elements of Math Workshop so you can capture what is being said and done. With them, you will be able to give great feedback and plan for next steps!

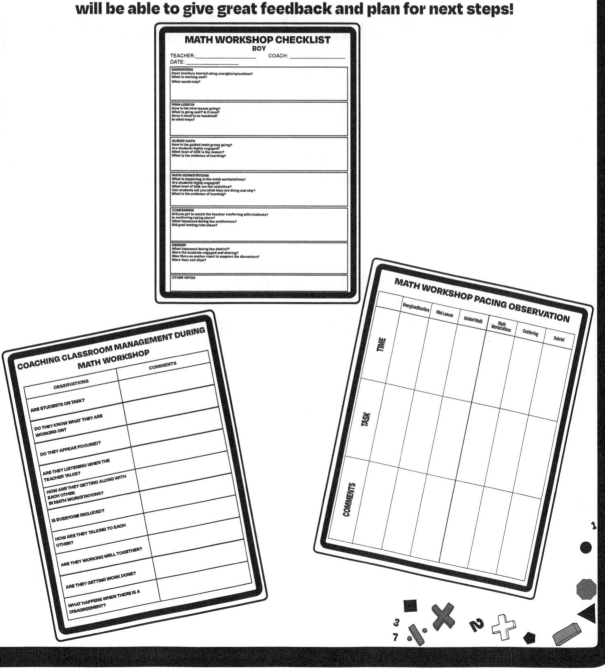

MATH WORKSHOP CHECKLIST
BOY

TEACHER: _____ COACH: _____
DATE: _____

ENERGIZERS
Have teachers started using energizers/routines?
What is working well?
What needs help?

MINI-LESSON
How is the mini-lesson going?
What is going well? Is it mini?
Does it need to be tweaked?
In what ways?

GUIDED MATH
How is the guided math group going?
Are students highly engaged?
What level of DOK is the lesson?
What is the evidence of learning?

MATH WORKSTATIONS
What is happening in the math workstations?
Are students highly engaged?
What level of DOK are the activities?
Can students tell you what they are doing and why?
What is the evidence of learning?

CONFERRING
Did you get to watch the teacher conferring with students?
Is conferring taking place?
What happened during the conference?
Did goal-setting take place?

DEBRIEF
What happened during the debrief?
Were the students engaged and sharing?
Was there an anchor chart to support the discussion?
Were their exit slips?

OTHER NOTES

COACHING CLASSROOM MANAGEMENT DURING MATH WORKSHOP

OBSERVATIONS	COMMENTS
ARE STUDENTS ON TASK?	
DO THEY KNOW WHAT THEY ARE WORKING ON?	
DO THEY APPEAR FOCUSED?	
ARE THEY LISTENING WHEN THE TEACHER TALKS?	
HOW ARE THEY GETTING ALONG WITH EACH OTHER IN MATH WORKSTATIONS?	
IS EVERYONE INCLUDED?	
HOW ARE THEY TALKING TO EACH OTHER?	
ARE THEY WORKING WELL TOGETHER?	
ARE THEY GETTING WORK DONE?	
WHAT HAPPENS WHEN THERE IS A DISAGREEMENT?	

MATH WORKSHOP PACING OBSERVATION

	Energizer/Routine	Mini Lesson	Guided Math	Math Workstations	Conferring	Debrief
TIME						
TASK						
COMMENTS						

Coaching Math Workshop

Looks Like

Sounds Like

Feels Like

I Wonder...

MATH WORKSHOP CHECKLIST
BOY

TEACHER:_____   COACH: _____

DATE: _____

ENERGIZERS/ROUTINES
Have teachers started using energizers/routines?
What is working well?
What needs help?

MINI-LESSON
How is the mini-lesson going?
What is going well? Is it mini?
Does it need to be tweaked?
In what ways?

GUIDED MATH
How is the guided math group going?
Are students highly engaged?
What level of DOK is the lesson?
What is the evidence of learning?

MATH WORKSTATIONS
What is happening in the math workstations?
Are students highly engaged?
What level of DOK are the activities?
Can students tell you what they are doing and why?
What is the evidence of learning?

CONFERRING
Did you get to watch the teacher conferring with students?
Is conferring taking place?
What happened during the conference?
Did goal-setting take place?

DEBRIEF
What happened during the debrief?
Were the students engaged and sharing?
Was there an anchor chart to support the discussion?
Were there exit slips?

OTHER NOTES

MATH WORKSHOP CHECKLIST
MOY

TEACHER:_____   COACH: _____

DATE: _____

ENERGIZERS/ROUTINES
Is the teacher using energizers/routines?
What is working well?
What needs help?

MINI-LESSON
How is the mini-lesson going?
What is going well? Is it mini?
Does it need to be tweaked?
In what ways?

GUIDED MATH
How is the guided math group going?
Are students highly engaged?
What level of DOK is the lesson?
What is the evidence of learning?

MATH WORKSTATIONS
What is happening in the math workstations?
Are students highly engaged?
What level of DOK are the activities?
Can students tell you what they are doing and why?
What is the evidence of learning?

CONFERRING
Did you get to watch the teacher conferring with students?
Is conferring taking place?
What happened during the conference?
Did goal-setting take place?

DEBRIEF
What happened during the debrief?
Were the students engaged and sharing?
Was there an anchor chart to support the discussion?
Were there exit slips?

OTHER NOTES

MATH WORKSHOP CHECKLIST
EOY

TEACHER:_____   COACH: _____

DATE: _____

ENERGIZERS/ROUTINES
Is the teacher using energizers/routines?
What is working well?
What needs help?

MINI-LESSON
How is the mini-lesson going?
What is going well?
Is it mini? Does it need to be tweaked?
In what ways?

GUIDED MATH
How is the guided math group going?
Are students highly engaged?
What level of DOK is the lesson?
What is the evidence of learning?

MATH WORKSTATIONS
What is happening in the math workstations?
Are students highly engaged?
What level of DOK are the activities?
Can students tell you what they are doing and why?
What is the evidence of learning?

CONFERRING
Did you get to watch the teacher conferring with students?
Is conferring taking place?
What happened during the conference?
Did goal-setting take place?

DEBRIEF
What happened during the debrief?
Were the students engaged and sharing?
Was there an anchor chart to support the discussion?
Were there exit slips?

OTHER NOTES

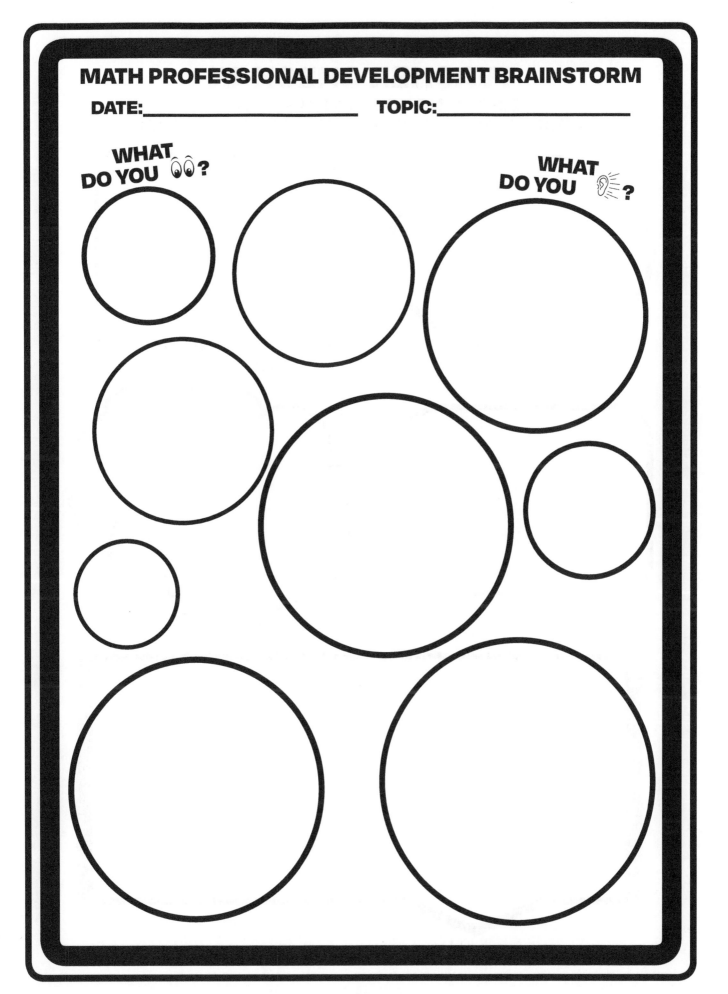

MATH PROFESSIONAL DEVELOPMENT BRAINSTORM

DATE:_____ TOPIC:_____

WHAT DO YOU 👀?

WHAT DO YOU 👂?

TEACHER CHECK-IN
LISTENING TO MATH DISCOURSE
RECORD WHAT YOU HEAR IN THE CLASSROOM

TEACHER CHECK-IN

WHAT DID YOU SEE, HEAR, NOTICE AND WONDER?

Teacher: _____   Date: _____

Coach: _____   Time: _____

SEE, HEAR, NOTICE, WONDER

CIRCLE COMPONENTS OBSERVED
Energizer, Mini-Lesson, Guided Math, Math Workstations, Conferring and Debrief

CLASSROOM SNAPSHOTS

Teacher: _____

Coach: _____

Date: _____

Time: _____

What do you see?

What do you hear?

What are students doing?

CLASSROOM SNAPSHOTS

Teacher: _____   **Date:** _____

Coach: _____   **Time:** _____

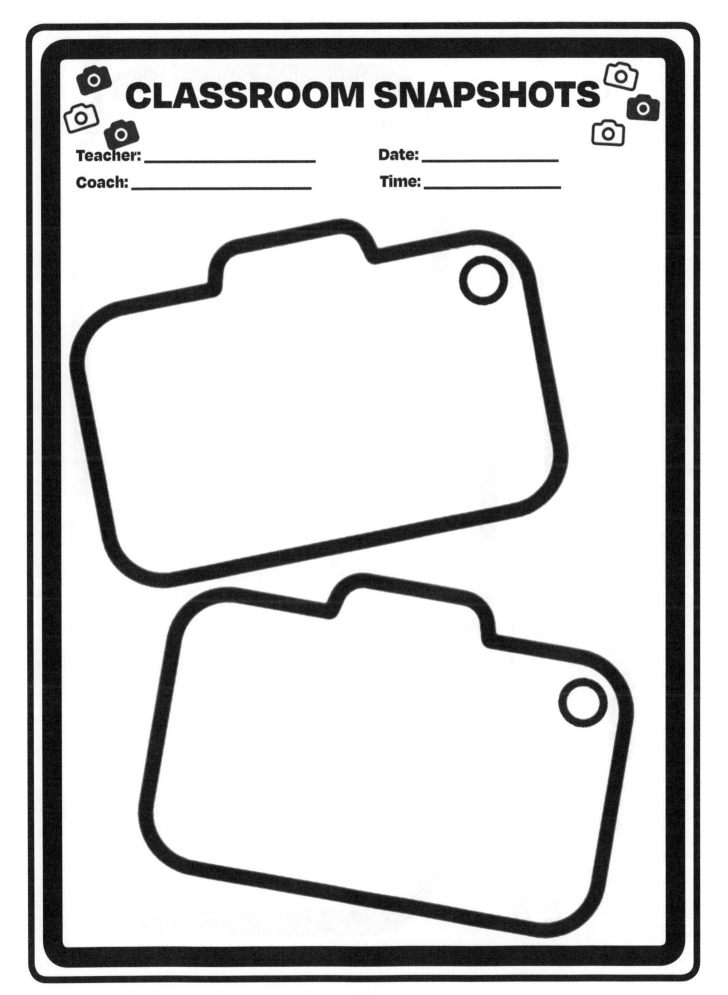

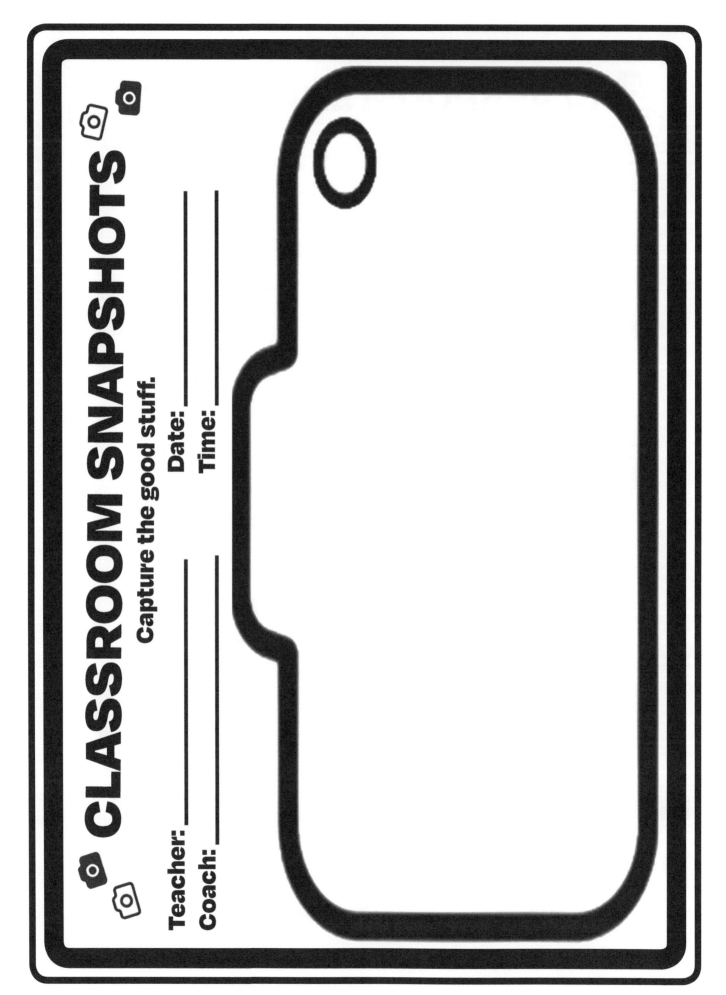

CLASSROOM SNAPSHOTS

Capture the good stuff.

Teacher: _____

Coach: _____

Date: _____

Time: _____

CLASSROOM SNAPSHOTS

Teacher: _____   **Date:** _____

Coach: _____   **Time:** _____

Capture the important moments

CLASSROOM SNAPSHOTS

Teacher: _____

Coach: _____

Date: _____

Time: _____

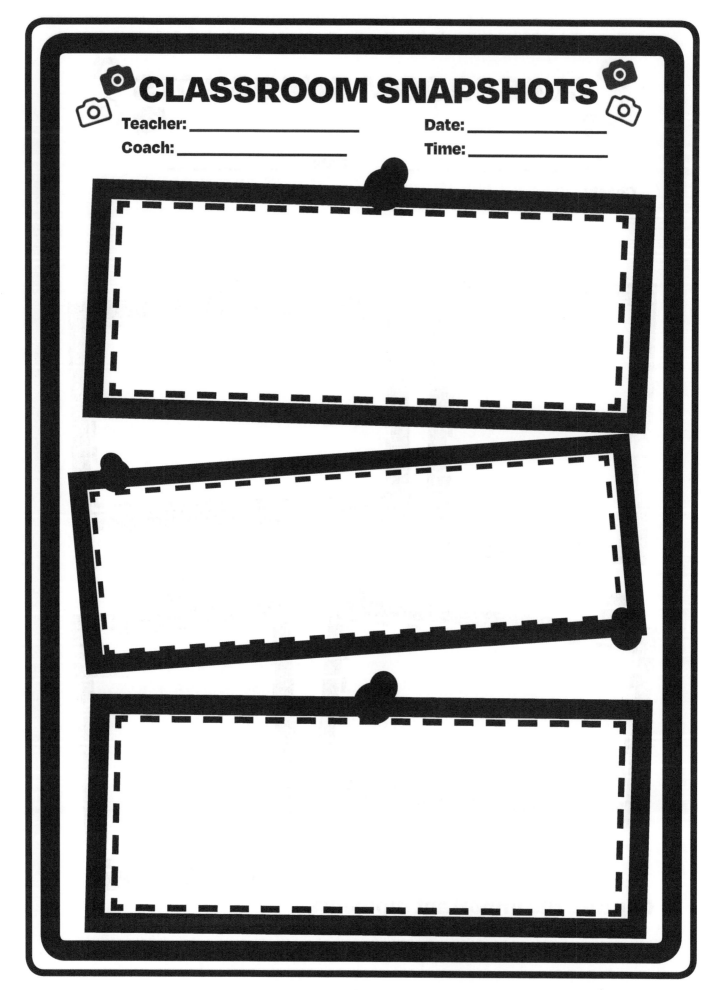

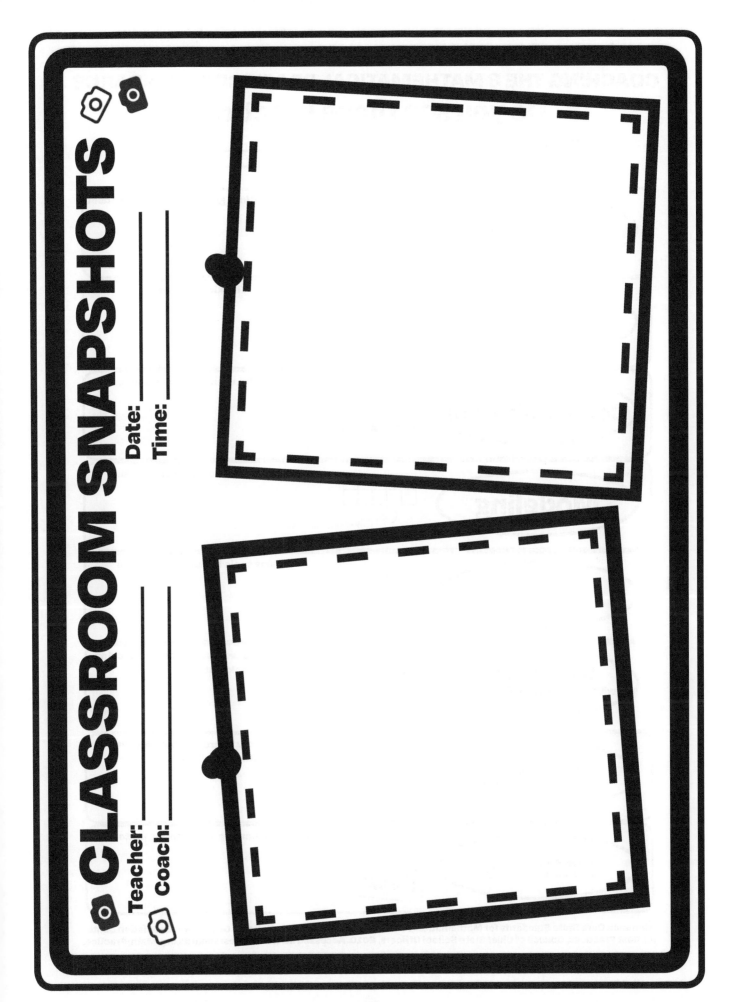

CLASSROOM SNAPSHOTS

Teacher: _____

Coach: _____

Date: _____

Time: _____

COACHING THE 8 MATHEMATICAL PRACTICES STANDARDS
Do you see these in action?

Teacher:_____   Date: _____

Coach: _____   Time: _____

Perseverance — Keep trying/not giving up/Growth Mindset

Reasoning — Thinking logically

Communication — Reading, writing, talking and speaking about math

Modeling — Using models to represent thinking

Tools — Using tools to think about math

Precision (with language and calculations) — Using the precise words and double checking calculations

Product
$3 \times 7 = 21$

Structure — Understanding how to break apart and put together numbers

$24 = 20 + 4$

$\frac{5}{4} = \frac{2}{4} + \frac{3}{4}$

Patterns — Seeking, recognizing, naming and creating patterns

$2,4,6,8$

"Common Core State Standards for Mathematical Practice." Washington, D.C.: National Governors Association Center for Best Practices, Council of Chief State School Officers, 2010. Accessed at: www.corestandards.org/Math/Practice.

TAKING A CLOSER LOOK
Math Workstations

Teacher:_____   Date: _____
Coach: _____   Time: _____

What are students doing?

What are students saying?

What is the evidence that students are learning?

Are the learning goals and success criteria clear?

Are the math workstations differentiated?

TAKING A CLOSER LOOK
Energizers and Routines

Teacher:_____   Date: _____
Coach: _____   Time: _____

What are students saying?

Are all the students engaged?

What is the evidence that students are learning?

What are students doing?

TAKING A CLOSER LOOK
Guided Math

Teacher:_____

Coach: _____

Date: _____

Time: _____

What are students doing? Do they have manipulatives?

What are students saying?

In what ways is the lesson scaffolded?

How long did the lesson take?

Are the learning goals and success criteria clear?

How were the students chosen for this group?

What is the evidence that students are learning?

TAKING A CLOSER LOOK
Mini-Lesson

Teacher:_____
Coach: _____

Date: _____
Time: _____

What are students saying?

Did the teacher co-create or use an anchor chart with the students?

How long did the mini-lesson take?

What are students doing?

Are the learning goals and success criteria clear?

TAKING A CLOSER LOOK
Debrief

Teacher:_____
Coach: _____

Date: _____
Time: _____

What are the students doing?

What are students saying?

What is the evidence that the students attained the learning goals success criteria?

In what ways are the students talking about what they have learned?

TAKING A CLOSER LOOK

Teacher:_____   Date: _____
Coach: _____   Time: _____

RECORD: WHAT'S HAPPENING?
CAPTURE 5 SCENES FROM THE CLASSROOM!

Teacher: _____

Coach: _____

Date: _____

Time: _____

RECORD: WHAT'S HAPPENING?
CAPTURING SCENES FROM THE CLASSROOM!

Teacher: _____

Coach: _____

Date: _____

Time: _____

RECORD: WHAT'S HAPPENING?
CAPTURING SCENES FROM THE CLASSROOM!

Teacher: _____
Coach: _____

Date: _____
Time: _____

RECORD: WHAT'S HAPPENING?
CAPTURING SCENES FROM THE CLASSROOM!

Teacher: _____

Coach: _____

Date: _____

Time: _____

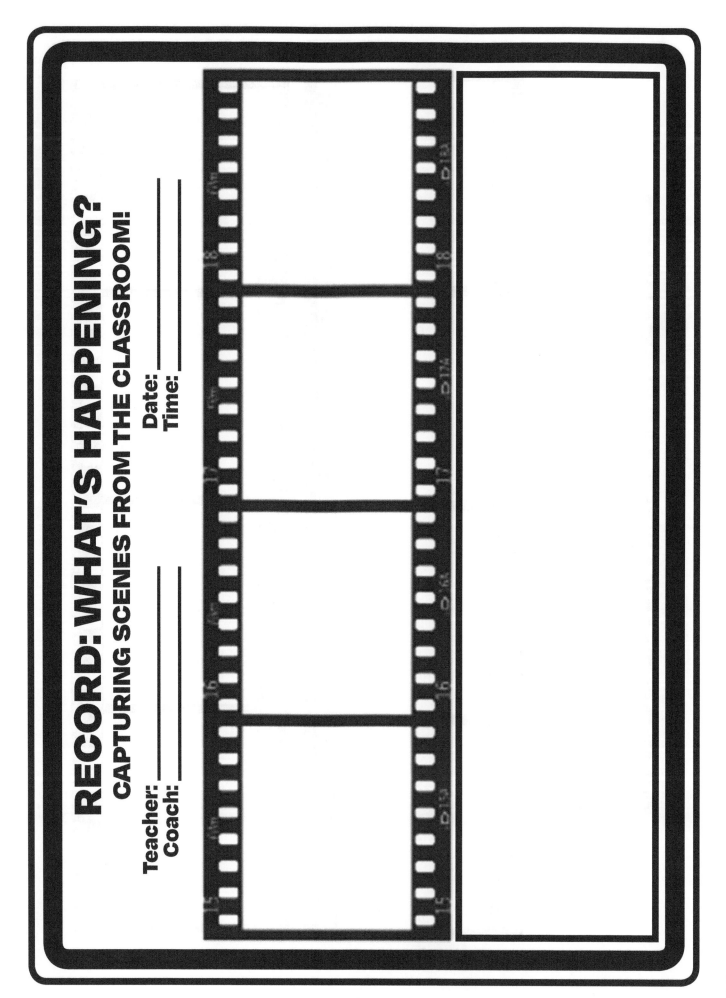

RECORD: WHAT'S HAPPENING?
CAPTURING SCENES FROM THE CLASSROOM!

Teacher: _____
Coach: _____

Date: _____
Time: _____

Math Workshop Observation

Teacher : _____   Date :_____

Coach : _____   Time :_____

Math Workshop Components Observed
(Circle components)

Energizer/Routine   Math Workstations

Mini-Lesson   Conferring

Guided Math   Debrief

Math Vocabulary

Conversations   Word Wall

Anchor Charts   Teaching

Language Frames

Evidence of Learning

Informal   Formal

Oral   Written

Rubrics

Engagement

Highly Engaged   Somewhat Engaged

Disengaged

TEACHER VISITS/CHECK-INS

Teacher	Energizer Routine	Mini-Lessons	Guided Math	Math Workstations	Conferring	Debrief	Transition	Classroom Management

MATH WORKSHOP OBSERVATIONS

Coach:

Teacher:

Date:

Component:

Coach:

Teacher:

Date:

Component:

Coach:

Teacher:

Date:

Component:

Coach:

Teacher:

Date:

Component:

FOCUSED MATH WORKSHOP VISIT

TEACHER: _____   DATE:_____

COACH: _____   TIME:_____

SUBJECT/LESSON:_____

ON WHAT PART OF MATH WORKSHOP DID YOU FOCUS?

ENERGIZER/ROUTINES   MATH WORKSTATIONS

MINI-LESSON   CONFERRING

GUIDED MATH   DEBRIEF

                                                        OTHER _____

What did you see? What was the teacher doing? What were the students doing?	Was the learning target and the success criteria evident?
What did you hear? **What were the students saying?** **What did the teacher say?**	**What do you wonder?**

MATH WORKSHOP PACING

	Energizer/Routine	Mini-Lesson	Guided Math	Math Workstations	Conferring	Debrief
COMMENTS						
TIME SPENT						
TASK						

FOCUSED MATH WORKSHOP VISIT
TIME MANAGEMENT

TEACHER: _____   DATE:_____

COACH: _____   TIME:_____

SUBJECT/LESSON OBSERVED:_____

ENERGIZER/ ROUTINE	MINI-LESSON	GUIDED MATH GROUP	MATH WORKSHOP	DEBRIEF
TIME	TIME	TIME	TIME	TIME
WHAT HAPPENED?	WHAT HAPPENED?	WHAT HAPPENED?	WHAT HAPPENED?	WHAT HAPPENED?
TOO LITTLE TOO MUCH JUST RIGHT	TOO LITTLE TOO MUCH JUST RIGHT	TOO LITTLE TOO MUCH JUST RIGHT	TOO LITTLE TOO MUCH JUST RIGHT	TOO LITTLE TOO MUCH JUST RIGHT

NOTICINGS

WONDERINGS

Coaching Notes

COACH :_____   **TEACHER:**_____

DATE: _____

Math Workshop Focus

Evidence of Learning

Differentiation

Vocabulary

Additional Notes/Thoughts

GENERAL WALKTHROUGH

Teacher: _____   Date: _____

Coach: _____

WHAT TO LOOK FOR:

☐ **PHYSICAL ENVIRONMENT**   ☐ **ACADEMIC ENVIRONMENT**   ☐ **EMOTIONAL/SOCIAL ENVIRONMENT**

- WHOLE GROUP SPACE
- GUIDED MATH SPACE
- WORKSTATIONS
- TOOLS AND TEMPLATES
- MANIPULATIVES
- WORD WALLS

- MATH TALK
- STUDENT CHOICE
- ENGAGEMENT
- RICH MATH TASKS
- PACING
- DIFFERENTIATION

- SENSE OF BELONGING
- PEER RELATIONSHIPS
- JOY
- WONDER
- CREATIVITY
- STUDENT/TEACHER RELATIONSHIPS
- STUDENT/STUDENT RELATIONSHIPS

GLOWS: **GROWS:**

WONDERINGS:

COACHING FORM

Teacher: _____

Coach: _____

Date: _____

WHAT DO YOU SEE?

WHAT DO YOU HEAR?

WHAT DO YOU FEEL?

WHAT DO YOU WONDER?

WHAT DO YOU SUGGEST?

COACHING FORM

Teacher: _____

Coach: _____

Date: _____

WHAT DO YOU SEE?

WHAT DO YOU HEAR?

WHAT DO YOU FEEL?

FOCUSED MATH WORKSHOP PRE-CONFERENCE

Teacher: _____   Date :_____

Coach: _____   Time :_____

Component Coached: _____

Goal 1:	Evidence of implementation
Goal 2:	Evidence of implementation
Goal 3:	Evidence of implementation
Follow up Date: **Notes:**	

Pre-Conference Notes

Teacher: _____

Coach: _____

Date : _____

Time : _____

Math Workshop Focus

Evidence of Learning

Differentiation

Materials

Other Comments

Coaching Math Workshop Pre-Conference Questions

Content:

What is your overall goal?

Which standards will you address in this lesson?

What part of Math Workshop will you be doing this lesson?

Which mathematical practices will you focus on in the lesson?

What do you anticipate will go really well?

Where do you anticipate any challenges? What have you planned to do to address them?

Assessment:

Will you be doing a pre-assessment?

How will you know if students have learned it?

Will you be giving an exit slip?

How will you assess for understanding throughout the lesson?

Differentiation:

How will you differentiate the lesson? What types of scaffolding will there be throughout the lesson?

Coaching:

What would you like me to help you with?

With which aspect do you feel you need coaching?

PRE-CONFERENCE PLANNING SHEET

Teacher: _____

Date: _____

Grade: _____

Essential Question	Learning Goal	Success Criteria

Math Workshop Component	Differentiation	Data Sources

Engagement Strategy	Resources

FOCUSED MATH WORKSHOP
PRE-PLANNING CONFERENCE

TEACHER: _____   DATE:_____

COACH: _____   TIME:_____

SUBJECT/LESSON OBSERVED:_____

ON WHAT PART OF MATH WORKSHOP WILL YOU FOCUS?	
ENERGIZER/ROUTINES	MATH WORKSTATIONS
MINI-LESSON	CONFERRING
GUIDED MATH	DEBRIEF
	OTHER _____

What will we see? What will the teacher be doing? What will the students be doing?	How will the learning target and the success criteria be evident?
What will you hear? What will the students be discussing? What will the teacher say?	What do you wonder?

FOCUSED CLASSROOM VISIT
ENERGIZER/ROUTINE

TEACHER: _____   DATE:_____

COACH: _____   TIME:_____

What was the goal of the energizer/routine?

Why was this energizer/routine selected?

Were the students participating? How?

What questions were being asked? By whom?

What was the evidence that students were learning?

MATH ENERGIZERS AND ROUTINES
Reflection Sheet

	Energizers and Routines	Check-ins/ Coaching Sessions
Monday		
Tuesday		
Wednesday		
Thursday		
Friday		

What is going well?

What do you need to change?

What evidence of student learning do you have?

FOCUSED CLASSROOM VISIT
MINI-LESSON

TEACHER: _____   **DATE:**_____

COACH: _____   **TIME:**_____

What was the goal of the mini-lesson?

Why was this selected?

Were the students participating? How?

What questions were being asked? By whom?

What tools and templates were used during the mini-lesson?

What was the evidence that students were learning?

FOCUSED CLASSROOM VISIT
GUIDED MATH GROUP

TEACHER: _____   DATE:_____

COACH: _____   TIME:_____

What was the goal of the guided group?

Why was this guided math lesson selected?

Were the students participating? How?

What scaffolds were used throughout the lesson?

How was the language scaffolded in the lesson?

Was the learning target and success criteria evident?

What questions were being asked? By whom?

What was the evidence that students were learning?

What was the level of rigor in the lesson?

Were students actively engaged?

Coaching Math Workshop
Guided Math Planning Sheet

Teacher : _____   Week :_____

Group 1	Group 2

Group 3	Group 4

Coaching Math Workshop
Guided Math Planning Sheet

Teacher : _____   Week :_____

	Group 1	Group 2	Group 3	Group 4
Monday	What? Why?	What? Why?	What? Why?	What? Why?
Tuesday	What? Why?	What? Why?	What? Why?	What? Why?
Wednesday	What? Why?	What? Why?	What? Why?	What? Why?
Thursday	What? Why?	What? Why?	What? Why?	What? Why?
Friday	What? Why?	What? Why?	What? Why?	What? Why?

Coaching Math Workshop

Guided Math Planning Sheet

Teacher : _____   Week :_____

	Group 1	Group 2	Group 3	Group 4
Monday	What? What's next?	What? What's next?	What? What's next?	What? What's next?
Tuesday	What? What's next?	What? What's next?	What? What's next?	What? What's next?
Wednesday	What? What's next?	What? What's next?	What? What's next?	What? What's next?
Thursday	What? What's next?	What? What's next?	What? What's next?	What? What's next?
Friday	What? What's next?	What? What's next?	What? What's next?	What? What's next?

Coaching Math Workshop

Guided Math Planning Sheet

Teacher : _____   Week :_____

	Group 1	Group 2	Group 3	Group 4
Monday				
Tuesday				
Wednesday				
Thursday				
Friday				

FOCUSED MATH WORKSHOP VISIT
MATH WORKSTATIONS

TEACHER: _____   **DATE:** _____

COACH: _____   **TIME:** _____

What was the goal of the workstations?

How were students assigned to the workstations?

Were the stations differentiated?

Were the students participating? How?

What was the evidence that students were learning?

What was the level of rigor in the workstations?

Were students actively engaged?

MATH WORKSTATIONS

Day	Math Workstation	Reason
Monday		
Tuesday		
Wednesday		
Thursday		
Friday		

What is going well?

What do you need to change?

What evidence of student learning do you have?

FOCUSED MATH WORKSHOP VISIT

LOOKING AT MATH WORKSTATIONS

TEACHER: _____   DATE:_____

COACH: _____   TIME:_____

What was the goal of the workstations?

How were students assigned to the workstations?

Were the stations differentiated?

Were the students participating? How?

What was the level of rigor in the workstations?

What was the evidence that students were learning?

Were students actively engaged?

FOCUSED MATH WORKSHOP VISIT

DEBRIEF

TEACHER: _____   DATE: _____

COACH: _____   TIME: _____

What was the goal of the debrief?

How did students participate in the debrief?

What was the evidence that students were learning?

Were students actively engaged? How?

FOCUSED MATH WORKSHOP VISIT
STUDENT DISCOURSE

TEACHER: _____   DATE:_____

COACH: _____   TIME:_____

SUBJECT/LESSON OBSERVED:_____

What were the norms for participation? (equity sticks, hand-raising, wheel of names etc.)

Who participated the most?

Who participated the least?

How were students encouraged to participate?

Noticings: _____
_____
_____
_____

Wonderings: _____
_____
_____
_____
_____

FOCUSED MATH WORKSHOP VISIT
MATH VOCABULARY

TEACHER: _____   **DATE:** _____

COACH: _____   **TIME:** _____

SUBJECT/LESSON OBSERVED: _____

How is language used in the classroom?

Is there an illustrated word wall?

In what ways is the math vocabulary used in the mini-lesson?

In what ways is the math vocabulary used in guided math groups?

In what ways is the math vocabulary used in math workstations?

In what ways is the math vocabulary used in the debrief?

Did you hear the teacher using math vocabulary?

Did you hear the students using math vocabulary?

Noticings: _____
_____
_____
_____

Wonderings: _____
_____
_____
_____
_____

Math Workshop Teacher Questioning

1. What types of questions did the teacher ask?

☐ Open
☐ Closed

Dok Level
☐ 1 ☐ 2 ☐ 3

Blooms Taxonomy: Remember, Understand, Apply, Analyze, Evaluate, Create

NOTES:

2. What types of questions did the students ask?

Teacher Questioning
What Questions Is the Teacher Asking?

DOK Level _____
☐ 1 ☐ 2 ☐ 3

Bloom's type _____
remembering, understanding, applying,
analyzing, evaluating, creating

☐ Open
☐ Closed

Notes

Are both the teacher and students asking questions?

Are students asking each other questions?

How are students answering the questions?

What else stands out?

Math Workshop Focused Coaching
What Types of Learning Are Students Being Asked to Do?

TEACHER: _____   DATE: _____

COACH: _____   TIME: _____

CREATE
Produce new or original work

EVALUATE
Justify a stand or desicion

ANALYZE
Draw connections among ideas

APPLY
Use information in new situations

UNDERSTAND
Explain ideas or concepts

REMEMBER
Recall facts and basic concepts

*Anderson, L.W. (Ed.), Krathwohl, D.R. (Ed.), Airasian, P.W., Cruikshank, K.A., Mayer, R.E., Pintrich, P.R., Raths, J., & Wittrock, M.C. (2001). *A taxonomy for learning, teaching, and assessing: A revision of Bloom's Taxonomy of Educational Objectives* (Complete edition). New York: Longman.

Math Workshop Focused Coaching

What Types of Thinking Are Students Being Asked to Do?

TEACHER: _____

COACH: _____

DATE: _____

TIME: _____

CREATE

EVALUATE

ANALYZE

APPLY

UNDERSTAND

REMEMBER

*Anderson, L.W. (Ed.), Krathwohl, D.R. (Ed.), Airasian, P.W., Cruikshank, K.A., Mayer, R.E., Pintrich, P.R., Raths, J., & Wittrock, M.C. (2001). *A taxonomy for learning, teaching, and assessing: A revision of Bloom's Taxonomy of Educational Objectives* (Complete edition). New York: Longman.

Math Workshop Focused Coaching Engagement

TEACHER: _____   **DATE:** _____

COACH: _____   **TIME:** _____

ENGAGEMENT: HIGH ATTENTION-HIGH COMMITMENT

STRATEGIC COMPLIANCE: HIGH ATTENTION-LOW COMMITMENT

RITUAL COMPLIANCE: LOW ATTENTION-LOW COMMITMENT

RETREATISM: NO ATTENTION-NO COMMITMENT

REBELLION: DIVERTED ATTENTION-NO COMMITMENT

*SCHLECHTY, P. (2002). *WORKING ON THE WORK*. SAN FRANCISCO: JOSSEY-BASS.

Math Workshop Focused Observation Engagement

TEACHER: _____   **DATE:** _____

COACH: _____   **TIME:** _____

ENGAGEMENT: HIGH ATTENTION-HIGH COMMITMENT
Student is paying attention, learning and interested.

STRATEGIC COMPLIANCE: HIGH ATTENTION-LOW COMMITMENT
Student is paying attention but isn't very interested.

RITUAL COMPLIANCE: LOW ATTENTION-LOW COMMITMENT
Student is paying attention because s/he is expected to. The participation is compliance-driven. Student wants to avoid a negative consequence.

RETREATISM: NO ATTENTION-NO COMMITMENT
Student is not paying attention, not participating but not disruptive.

REBELLION: DIVERTED ATTENTION-NO COMMITMENT
Student is not paying attention, not interested and doing other things that can be distracting and disruptive to other students' learning.

*SCHLECHTY, P. (2002). *WORKING ON THE WORK.* SAN FRANCISCO: JOSSEY-BASS.

Math Workshop Focused Coaching Engagement

TEACHER: _____   **DATE:** _____
COACH: _____   **TIME:** _____

ENGAGEMENT: HIGH ATTENTION-HIGH COMMITMENT
Student is paying attention, learning and interested.

REBELLION: DIVERTED ATTENTION-NO COMMITMENT
Student is not paying attention, not interested and doing other things that can be distracting and disruptive to other students' learning.

STRATEGIC COMPLIANCE: HIGH ATTENTION-LOW COMMITMENT
Student is paying attention but isn't very interested.

RETREATISM: NO ATTENTION - NO COMMITMENT
Student is not paying attention, not participating but not disruptive.

RITUAL COMPLIANCE: LOW ATTENTION-LOW COMMITMENT
Student is paying attention because s/he is expected to. The participation is compliance-driven. Student wants to avoid a negative consequence.

*SCHLECHTY, P. (2002). *WORKING ON THE WORK*. SAN FRANCISCO: JOSSEY-BASS.

Math Workshop Math Talk Coaching Session

Who is talking?

_____ (Number of Boys) _____ (Number of Girls)

_____ (Number of IEP) _____ (Number of Emergent Bilinguals)

What are they saying?

Are students talking to each other?

Is the teacher encouraging/facilitating student to student conversation?

What scaffolds are set up to help students use academic language? (language stems, math vocabulary)

Notice who is talking most. Boys or girls?

How are the Emergent Bilinguals engaging in the conversation?

Math Workshop Math Talk Coaching Session

Who is talking?

What are students saying?

Are students talking to each other?

Is the teacher encouraging/facilitating student to student conversation?

What scaffolds are set up to help students use academic language? (language stems, math vocabulary)

Notice who is talking most. Boys or girls?

How are the Emergent Bilinguals engaging in the conversation?

COACHING CLASSROOM MANAGEMENT DURING MATH WORKSHOP

NOTICINGS	COMMENTS
ARE STUDENTS ON TASK?	
DO STUDENTS KNOW WHAT THEY ARE LEARNING?	
DO STUDENTS APPEAR FOCUSED?	
ARE STUDENTS LISTENING WHEN THE TEACHER TALKS?	
HOW ARE STUDENTS GETTING ALONG WITH EACH OTHER IN MATH WORKSTATIONS?	
ARE ALL STUDENTS INCLUDED?	
HOW ARE STUDENTS TALKING TO EACH OTHER?	
ARE STUDENTS WORKING WELL TOGETHER?	
ARE STUDENTS GETTING WORK DONE?	
WHAT HAPPENS WHEN THERE IS A DISAGREEMENT?	

FOCUSED MATH WORKSHOP VISIT

TEACHER: _____   DATE:_____

COACH: _____   TIME:_____

SUBJECT/LESSON OBSERVED:_____

What are you noticing about behaviors in Math Workshop?

What do you notice happens during the mini-lesson?

What happens during guided math groups?

Are students focused and on task during math workstation?

How are students acting during the debrief?

Are there any times when students are off task?

What could be the reasons that they are off task?

What suggestions do you have for them to be on task?

FOCUSED MATH WORKSHOP PRE-VISIT
BEHAVIOR

TEACHER: _____   DATE:_____

COACH: _____   TIME:_____

SUBJECT/LESSON OBSERVED:_____

What seems to be happening?

What are the behavior issues?

What is working?

What is not working?

What is kind of working?

What are the rules or community agreements?

What are the rewards and consequences?

How would the class be different if these behavior issues were resolved?

What would you like to do?

What do you think needs to be done?

FOCUSED MATH WORKSHOP PRE-VISIT
BEHAVIOR

TEACHER: _____   DATE:_____

  COACH: _____   TIME:_____

COMPONENT:_____

GOAL # 1	EVIDENCE OF IMPLEMENTATION

GOAL # 2	EVIDENCE OF IMPLEMENTATION

GOAL # 3	EVIDENCE OF IMPLEMENTATION

MATH WORKSHOP COACHING	MATH WORKSHOP COACHING
COACH: TEACHER: DATE: COMPONENT:	COACH: TEACHER: DATE: COMPONENT:
MATH WORKSHOP COACHING COACH: TEACHER: DATE: COMPONENT:	MATH WORKSHOP COACHING COACH: TEACHER: DATE: COMPONENT:

Focused Math Workshop Visit

Post-Visit Discussion

Teacher: _____   Date :_____

Coach: _____   Time :_____

What went well?

What would you do different?

How was the level of rigor?

How engaged were the students?

Was the lesson on grade level?

FOCUSED MATH WORKSHOP
POST VISIT

TEACHER: _____   **DATE:** _____

COACH: _____   **TIME:** _____

SUBJECT/LESSON: _____

WHAT PART OF MATH WORKSHOP DID YOU FOCUS ON?

ENERGIZER/ROUTINES	MATH WORKSTATIONS
MINI-LESSON	CONFERRING
GUIDED MATH	DEBRIEF
	OTHER _____

What went really well?

What should be tweaked?

What would you not do again?

What might be done differently next time?

FOCUSED MATH WORKSHOP
POST VISIT

TEACHER: _____   **DATE:** _____

COACH: _____   **TIME:** _____

SUBJECT/LESSON: _____

WHAT PART OF MATH WORKSHOP DID YOU FOCUS ON?	
ENERGIZER/ROUTINES	MATH WORKSTATIONS
MINI-LESSON	CONFERRING
GUIDED MATH	DEBRIEF
	OTHER _____

What did you see? Was the learning goal evident?	What did you hear?
What were the students doing? What was the teacher doing?	**What was the evidence of learning?**

Things to Do Next
Post Lesson Conference

TEACHER : _____   COACH:_____
DATE: _____

Coach	Teacher
COMPLETED ☐	COMPLETED ☐
COMPLETED ☐	COMPLETED ☐
COMPLETED ☐	COMPLETED ☐

Feedback

DOI: 10.4324/9781003458975-6

138

What You will Find in this Section!

In this section you will find different forms to help scaffold feedback conversations. Remember that feedback should be kind, helpful and action-oriented.

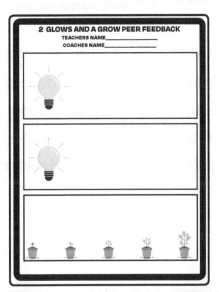

2 GLOWS AND A GROW PEER FEEDBACK

TEACHERS NAME_____

COACHES NAME_____

Feedback Form

	EVIDENCE	PARTIAL EVIDENCE	NO EVIDENCE YET
Evidence of Learning			
Differentiation			
Scaffolding			
Questioning			

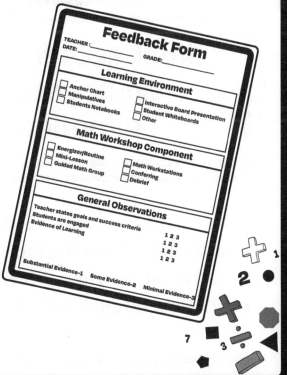

Feedback Form

TEACHER :_____
DATE:_____   GRADE:_____

Learning Environment

☐ Anchor Chart
☐ Manipulatives
☐ Students Notebooks
☐ Interactive Board Presentation
☐ Student Whiteboards
☐ Other

Math Workshop Component

☐ Energizer/Routine
☐ Mini-Lesson
☐ Guided Math Group
☐ Math Workstations
☐ Conferring
☐ Debrief

General Observations

Teacher states goals and success criteria   1 2 3
Students are engaged   1 2 3
Evidence of Learning   1 2 3
          1 2 3

Substantial Evidence-1   Some Evidence-2   Minimal Evidence-3

QUOTES

It is not what you say, it is how you say it!

Do you ever plan what you are going to say to teachers? Do you practice with one of your peer coaches to help make sure it is going to come out correctly? How do you say things? How do they land? After you talk with people, how do they feel?

"What gets feedback gets better. What gets coached, gets exponentially better."

How do the teachers at your school feel about feedback? Do people look forward to it or do they dread it? Why? How is it done? What is done really well? How could it be better?

*https://www.theprincipalsplaybook.com/instructional-leadership/instructional-feedback-coaching

QUOTES

"If your actions inspire others to dream more, learn more, do more and become more, you are a leader."

– John Quincy Adams

Does your feedback inspire, help teachers to dream, do more and become more? How? Name a few times that you have done this, this year, this month, today.....

"Teachers want to make a difference. The feedback they find most useful recognizes that commitment and, in collegial and supportive ways, helps them do just that" (Guskey & Link).

Does your feedback acknowledge the hard work and effort that teachers are doing everyday? Does your feedback feel supportive? After a feedback section how does everyone feel?

*Gusky,T. & Link, L.(n.d.) What Teachers Really Want When It Comes to Feedback retrieved on February 22 from https://www.ascd.org/el/articles/what-teachers-really-want-when-it-comes-to-feedback

"There is always space for improvement, no matter how long you've been in the business."

– Oscar De La Hoya

How do you work with veteran teachers?

"Words are singularly the most powerful force available to humanity. We can choose to use this force constructively with words of encouragement, or destructively using words of despair. Words have energy and power with the ability to help, to heal, to hinder, to hurt, to harm, to humiliate and to humble."

– Yehuda Berg

As coaches we must plan the words that come out of our mouths because they help shape the environments that we work in. Do you ever stop and reflect on the power of your words on any given day?

Feedback Cycle

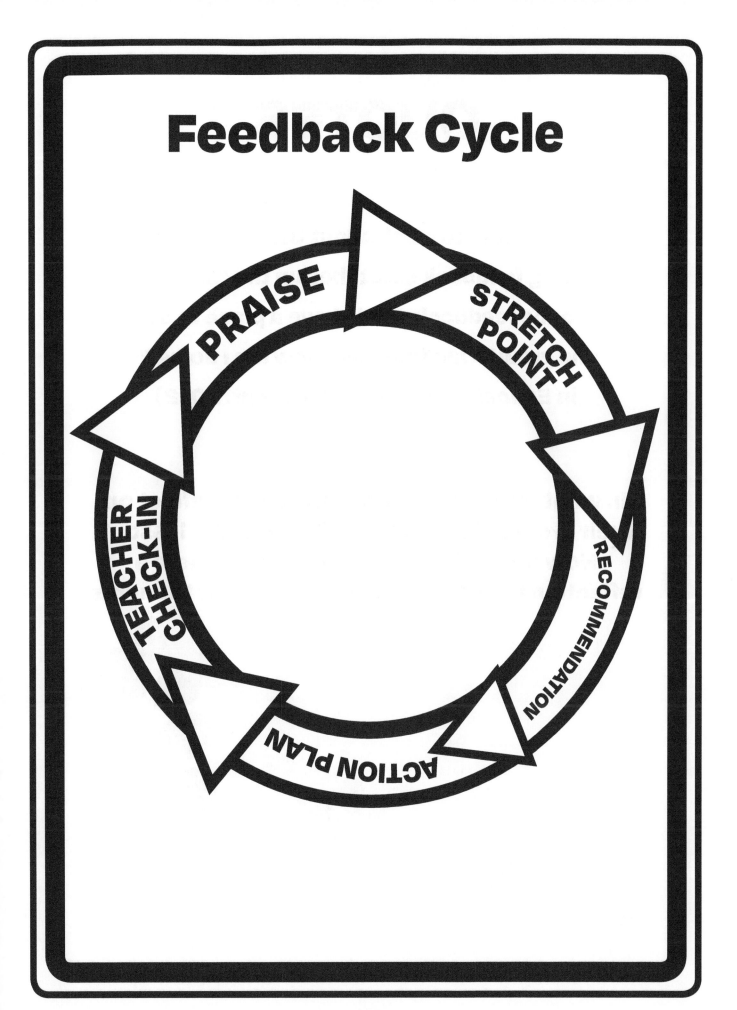

QUOTES

"Asking teachers to think about their practice before receiving feedback scratches up the "soil" in the brain so the feedback seeds have a place to settle in and grow." - Jan Chapuis "How am I doing?" in *Educational Leadership* (Sept. 2012)

In what ways do you get teachers to reflect on their process before you talk about the lesson? How do you have them reflect? Is there a reflection form for them to gather their thoughts before you talk?

Use this checklist to think about the feedback you give. Compare what you actually do with some of the main tenets of great feedback!

Criteria	Actual Feedback
BE AS SPECIFIC AS POSSIBLE	
INVITE TEACHER PARTICIPATION AND REFLECTION	
ADDRESS THE IMPACT ON STUDENT ACHIEVEMENT	
BE KIND AND HELPFUL	
GIVE IT AS SOON AS POSSIBLE	
BE ACTIONABLE	
BE FOLLOWED UP	

GOAL-REFERENCED

(tied to student achievement) (ties into district and school goals)

ACTIONABLE

concrete, specific and useful

TANGIBLE

anchor products, rubrics and exemplars

FEEDBACK SHOULD BE....

Teacher Friendly

Helpful

Ongoing Follow-Up

TIMELY

as immediate as possible

CONSISTENT

clear, accurate, trustworthy

Encouraging

THINGS YOU MIGHT SAY....

What is one big takeaway you have from this conversation?

...I noticed that your superpower is...

When you did that... it was great because....

You might think about this one small change... in order to improve student...

What went exactly as you had planned....?

In what ways does this connect with the district/ school goal of....?

If you were going to change anything...What would it be? Why?

What would you like to set as your next goal? Why? How will it improve student achievement?

Feedback Form

	EVIDENCE	PARTIAL EVIDENCE	NO EVIDENCE YET
Evidence of Learning			
Differentiation			
Scaffolding			
Questioning			

Feedback Form

TEACHER :_____   **GRADE:**_____
DATE: _____

Learning Environment

☐ Anchor Chart(s)   ☐ Interactive Board Presentation
☐ Manipulatives   ☐ Student Whiteboards
☐ Student Notebooks   ☐ Other
☐ Word Walls

Math Workshop Component

☐ Energizer/Routine   ☐ Math Workstations
☐ Mini-Lesson   ☐ Conferring
☐ Guided Math Group   ☐ Debrief

General Observations

Teacher states goals and success criteria   1 2 3
Students are engaged   1 2 3
Evidence of student learning   1 2 3

Substantial Evidence-1   Some Evidence-2   Minimal Evidence-3

Teacher Feedback Form

Teacher : _____   Date :_____

Coach : _____

Math Workshop Component: _____

_____
_____
_____
_____

Learning Environment	Math Workshop
☐ Math Bulletin Boards ☐ Anchor Charts ☐ Student Notebooks ☐ Rules and Procedures ☐ Other	What did I see? What did I hear? What did I wonder?

FEEDBACK CONFERENCES

Classroom Visit:

Coach:

Teacher:

Grade:

Coaching Assessment

Teacher/Date	Glows/Strengths	Grows

TWO GLOWS AND A GROW PEER FEEDBACK

TEACHER'S NAME:_____

COACH'S NAME:_____

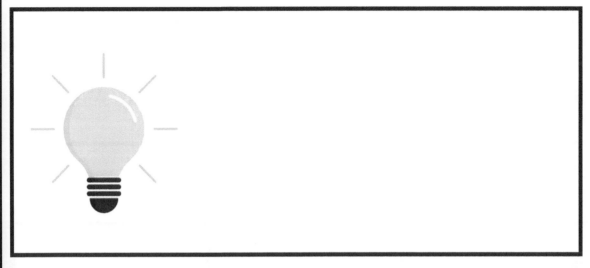

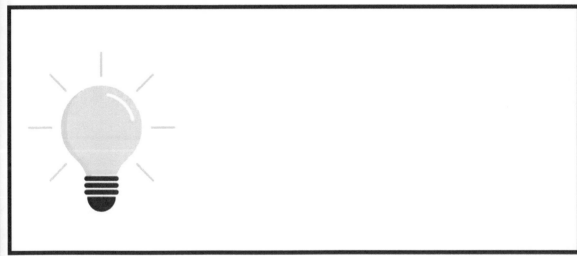

COACHING THE CLASSROOM ENVIRONMENT

Coach:

Teacher:

Grade:

	Glows/Strengths	Grows
Classroom routines & procedures		
Classroom rules/ consequences		
Classroom climate		
Student relationships and communication		
Sense of belonging		
Classroom jobs		
Cool down corner/ student regulation opportunities		
Promotion of Growth Mindset		

CLASSROOM ENVIRONMENT OBSERVATIONS

Coach:
Teacher:
Grade:

	Glows/Strengths	Grows
Classroom routines & procedures (ex. systems for going to the restroom, getting and sharpening pencils, getting drinks, getting/asking for help)		
Classroom transitions (ex. signals (multi-sensory) bells, songs, claps, chants, chimes, doorbells, windchimes)		
Classroom organization of student materials (folders, what do desks look like? how is work turned in?)		
Classroom rules/ consequences		
Classroom climate		
Student's relationships and communication		
Sense of belonging		
Classroom jobs		
Cool down corner/ student regulation opportunities		
Promotion of Growth Mindset		

Instructional Support Logs

DOI: 10.4324/9781003458975-7

What You will Find in this Section!

In this section you will find logs and keep track of general visits. These logs help you to know who, what and when you visited classrooms throughout the year! Keeping daily and weekly logs helps you to remember the support you provided during the week.

CLASSROOM VISIT

TEACHER: _____ DATE:_____
COACH:_____ TIME:_____

FOCUS OF VISIT:

ENERGIZER/ROUTINE   MATH WORKSTATIONS
MINI-LESSON   CONFERRING
GUIDED MATH   DEBRIEF

OBSERVATIONS: _____
_____
_____

WONDERINGS: _____
_____
_____

CLASSROOM VISIT

TEACHER: _____ DATE:_____
COACH:_____ TIME:_____

FOCUS OF VISIT:

ENERGIZER/ROUTINE   MATH WORKSTATIONS
MINI-LESSON   CONFERRING
GUIDED MATH   DEBRIEF

OBSERVATIONS: _____
_____
_____

WONDERINGS: _____
_____
_____

TEACHER SUPPORT

Teacher: _____
Grade: _____

DAY	ACTIVITY	COMPLETED/NEXT STEPS

TEACHER MEETINGS

TEACHER NAME/DATE	TOPIC DISCUSSED	NEXT STEPS

INSTRUCTIONAL SUPPORT LOG

COACH: _____
TEACHER: _____

Date: _____ **Initial Visit:** _____ **Follow up Completed:**
Follow up Visit: _____ _____

NOTES : _____
_____
_____
_____

WONDERINGS: _____
_____
_____
_____
_____

Date: _____ **Initial Visit:** _____ **Follow up Completed:**
Follow up Visit: _____ _____

NOTES : _____
_____
_____
_____

WONDERINGS: _____
_____
_____
_____
_____

Date: _____ **Initial Visit:** _____ **Follow up Completed:**
Follow up Visit: _____ _____

NOTES : _____
_____
_____

WONDERINGS: _____
_____
_____
_____

CLASSROOM VISIT LOG

Teachers	Dates									

CLASSROOM VISIT

TEACHER: _____   DATE:_____
COACH: _____   TIME:_____

FOCUS OF VISIT:

ENERGIZER/ROUTINE   MATH WORKSTATIONS
MINI-LESSON   CONFERRING
GUIDED MATH   DEBRIEF

NOTICINGS: _____
_____
_____

WONDERINGS: _____
_____
_____
_____

CLASSROOM VISIT

TEACHER: _____   DATE:_____
COACH: _____   TIME:_____

FOCUS OF VISIT:

ENERGIZER/ROUTINE   MATH WORKSTATIONS
MINI-LESSON   CONFERRING
GUIDED MATH   DEBRIEF

NOTICINGS: _____
_____
_____

WONDERINGS: _____
_____
_____
_____

CLASSROOM VISIT

TEACHER: _____   DATE:_____

COACH: _____   TIME:_____

FOCUS OF VISIT:

STUDENT BEHAVIOR   CLIMATE

PROCEDURES   PACING

CLASSROOM ENVIRONMENT   RULES/CONSEQUENCES

SCHEDULE   MATERIALS, TOOLS

NOTICINGS: _____

_____

_____

WONDERINGS: _____

_____

_____

CLASSROOM VISIT

TEACHER: _____   DATE:_____

COACH: _____   TIME:_____

FOCUS OF VISIT:

STUDENT BEHAVIOR   CLIMATE

PROCEDURES   PACING

CLASSROOM ENVIRONMENT   RULES/CONSEQUENCES

SCHEDULE   MATERIALS, TOOLS

NOTICINGS: _____

_____

_____

WONDERINGS: _____

_____

_____

CLASSROOM VISIT

TEACHER: _____   DATE:_____
COACH: _____   TIME:_____

FOCUS OF VISIT:

LESSON PLAN ALIGNMENT   QUESTIONING
TARGET GOAL   STUDENT DISCOURSE
SUCCESS CRITERIA   STUDENT ENGAGEMENT

NOTICINGS: _____
_____
_____
_____

WONDERINGS: _____
_____

CLASSROOM VISIT

TEACHER: _____   DATE:_____
COACH: _____   TIME:_____

FOCUS OF VISIT:

LESSON PLAN ALIGNMENT   QUESTIONING
TARGET GOAL   STUDENT DISCOURSE
SUCCESS CRITERIA   STUDENT ENGAGEMENT

NOTICINGS: _____
_____
_____
_____

WONDERINGS: _____
_____

COACHING CYCLE & CONFERENCE

COACH: _____

TEACHER: _____

Preconference Date: _____

Focus of Coaching Session: _____

NOTES : _____

_____

_____

_____

Observation Date: _____

Focus of Coaching Session: _____

NOTES : _____

_____

_____

_____

Post-Conference Date: _____

Focus of Conference: _____

Glows: _____   **Grows:** _____

_____   _____

_____   _____

_____   _____

_____   _____

_____   _____

_____   _____

Next Steps:

_____

_____

_____

_____

_____

TEACHER SUPPORT

Teacher: _____
Grade: _____

DAY	ACTIVITY	NEXT STEPS

TEACHER SUPPORT

Teacher: _____

Grade: _____

Beginning of the year notes	Middle of the year notes

End of the year notes	Notes for next year

TEACHER SUPPORT

Teacher: _____

Grade: _____

Beginning of the year notes	Middle of the year notes
Glows	Glows
Grows	Grows

End of the year notes	Other notes
Glows	Glows
Grows	Grows

TEACHER VISITS/OBSERVATIONS

TEACHER NAME	Aug	Sept	Oct	Nov	Dec	Jan	Feb	Mar	Apr	May	June

TEACHER VISITS/OBSERVATIONS

TEACHER NAME	DATES										

TEACHER MEETINGS

TEACHER NAME/DATE	TOPIC DISCUSSED	NEXT STEPS

TEACHER VISITS/CHECK-INS

TEACHER NAME	BOY	MOY	EOY

Coaching the Planning of Math Workshop

DOI: 10.4324/9781003458975-8

What You will Find in this Section!

In this section you will find forms to help teachers plan the different components of Math Workshop.

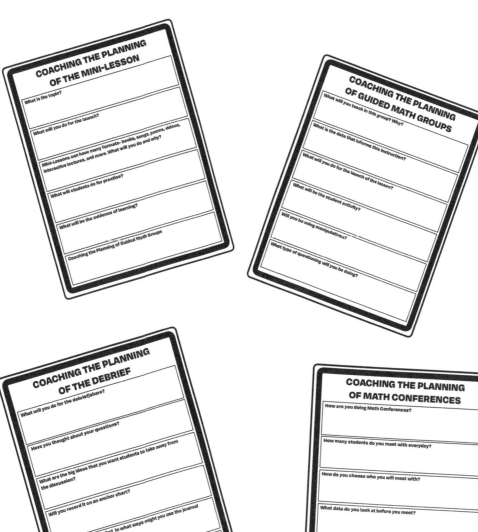

COACHING THE PLANNING OF THE MINI-LESSON

What is the topic?

What will you do for the launch?

Mini-Lessons can have many formats- books, songs, poems, videos, interactive lectures, and more. What will you do and why?

What will students do for practice?

What will be the evidence of learning?

Coaching the Planning of Guided Math Groups

COACHING THE PLANNING OF GUIDED MATH GROUPS

What will you teach in this group? Why?

What is the data that informs this instruction?

What will you do for the launch of the lesson?

What will be the student activity?

Will you be using manipulatives?

What type of questioning will you be doing?

COACHING THE PLANNING OF THE DEBRIEF

What will you do for the debrief/share?

Have you thought about your questions?

What are the big ideas that you want students to take away from the discussion?

Will you record it on an anchor chart?

What will be the exit slip? In what ways might you use the journal during the debrief?

How do students share their work with each other?

COACHING THE PLANNING OF MATH CONFERENCES

How are you doing Math Conferences?

How many students do you meet with everyday?

How do you choose who you will meet with?

What data do you look at before you meet?

Do you do goal setting during these conferences? If so, how do you follow-up?

Have you every done partner conferences?

COACHING THE PLANNING OF ENERGIZERS/ROUTINES

What energizers are you thinking about doing?

Why? What does the data say?

What are you doing for fluency energizers?

What are you doing for problem solving routines?

How do you plan for full engagement?

What do you have in place to scaffold access to the energizer for all students?

What is the evidence that students are learning the math?

COACHING THE PLANNING OF THE MINI-LESSON

What is the topic?

What will you do for the launch?

Mini-Lessons can have many formats - books, songs, poems, videos, interactive lectures and more. What will you do and why?

What will students do for practice?

What will be the evidence of learning?

What anchor chart(s) will support student learning?

COACHING THE PLANNING OF GUIDED MATH GROUPS

What will you teach in this group? Why?

What is the data that informs this instruction?

What will you do for the launch of the lesson?

What will be the student activity?

What manipulatives or templates are needed?

What types of questions will you use?

COACHING THE PLANNING OF GUIDED MATH GROUPS

Have you thought about questioning? Will you use some open and some closed questions? What level of Bloom's will you be using? What level of DOK are your questions?

What will the students do for guided work?

Will there be an exploration period?

What will be the independent work?

What will be the evidence that they have learned the math? How will you wrap up the lesson?

COACHING THE PLANNING OF WORKSTATIONS

How are you doing with the four Must-Have Workstations - fluency, place value, problem solving and the current unit of study?

In what ways will students be practicing - alone, partners or in small groups?

In what ways will the workstations be differentiated? How will you know that your students are on task?

What evidence of student learning will you monitor/assess?

COACHING THE PLANNING OF THE DEBRIEF

What will you do for the debrief?

Have you thought about your questions?

What are the big ideas that you want students to take away from the discussion?

How will you record the debrief?

What will be the exit slip? In what ways might you use the journal during the debrief?

How will students share their work with each other?

COACHING THE PLANNING OF MATH CONFERENCES

How are you doing Math Conferences?

How many students will you meet with every day?

How will you choose who you will meet with?

What data will you look at before you meet?

Do you do goal setting during these conferences? If so, how do you follow-up?

Coaching Plans, PD and Reflections

DOI: 10.4324/9781003458975-9

-What You will Find in this Section!

In this section there are many templates to set goals for the year, quarter, month and more. It is important to set goals, make action plans and then reflect on the achievement of those goals.

COACH REFLECTIONS
MOY

COACH: _____
DATE: _____

How is the year going overall?

What is going really well?

What is challenging? What can you do about it?

What is the trickiest part of what you do as a Math Coach?

Name 1-3 things you can celebrate this year so far!

What is a big goal for the next part of the year?

COACH REFLECTIONS
BOY

COACH: _____
DATE: _____

What do I want to do this year? Why?

What might be some challenges to doing this? How will I address these challenges?

What am I most excited about this year?

What do I want to get better at this year?

What part of Math Workshop do I know really well?

What part of Math Workshop do I want to get better at?

What part of Math Workshop do I need to know more about? How will I find out?

COACH REFLECTIONS
EOY

COACH: _____
DATE: _____

How was your year overall?

What went really well?

What do you need to work on for next year?

What was particularly challenging? Why?

Name 1-3 things you can celebrate this year!

What is a big goal for next year?

COACHING THE COACH

"DO THE BEST YOU CAN UNTIL YOU KNOW BETTER. THEN WHEN YOU KNOW BETTER, DO BETTER."

MAYA ANGELOU

HERE ARE 9 WAYS TO IMPROVE YOUR PRACTICE!

Show what you know: Present at a district, state or national conference

Become a member: Join a regional, state, or national organization

Write it Down: Write an article for a district, state, regional or national organization

Online Class: Take a course in something you want to know more about

Lead a Book Study: Facilitate a book study with other coaches or teachers to take a deep dive

Visit Schools: Visit other schools to get great ideas

Read or Start a Blog about Coaching

Social Media: Search or start a hashtag about teaching and learning math

Podcast: Join or start a podcast about teaching and learning math

(References: Literacy at Work, 2022; Fitzpatrick, 2022; Connecticut Department of Education

COACHING MENU

CHOOSE 3 WAYS YOU WOULD LIKE YOUR COACH TO HELP YOU THIS YEAR!

HERE ARE 9 OPTIONS FOR PD!

Demo a mini lesson

Demo a small group lesson

Finding Resources

Help with Math Workstations

Lead a Book Study

Setting up peer visits.

Demo the debrief

Co-teach a lesson

Demo an energizer/routine

Give me 2 numbers with a sum of 27.

Give me 2 numbers with a product of 50.

If the answer is 5, what is the question?"

(References: Literacy at Work, 2022; Fitzpatrick, 2022; Connecticut Department of Education

CHALLENGE YOURSELF

PICK AT LEAST 3-5 THINGS DURING THE SCHOOL YEAR THAT YOU WANT TO DO!
DO EVEN MORE IF YOU HAVE A CHANCE!

CATCH THEM BEING GREAT
(Do a post on social media about the great things that are happening)

PEER COACH A COACH
(Go and observe a coach coaching)

CO-PLAN A LESSON WITH A TEACHER
(Co-plan a lesson with a teacher)

COLLABORATION

CREATE A PD SURVEY OR QUESTIONNAIRE
(Create a survey or questionnaire to find out what teachers need)

CONDUCT MATH PD WITH PARAPROFESSIONALS
(Remember that paraprofessionals need training too!)

SHARE A MATH ARTICLE
(Find and share a Math Article worth reading)

STRETCH YOUR PEDAGOGY
(Try something new)

TRACK YOUR TIME
(Keep a log of a Day in your Coaching life)

CO-TEACH A LESSON
(Help a teacher with a lesson of their choice!)

READ A MATH PICTURE BOOK
(There are so many great math picture books - read 1)

CO-FACILITATE A FAMILY MATH DAY OR NIGHT
(Family events promote learning - do 1)

CELEBRATE SUCCESS WITH AN EMAIL
(Email 3 teachers a week with a celebration email)

VIDEO COACHING
(Catch yourself on camera)

DATA DIVE
(Be sure to look at data across a class, across grades, across grade bands and across the school)

OBSERVE A FULL MATH WORKSHOP
(At least once a week, try to observe a full math workshop session)

FOCUSED VISIT
(Spend a week looking at 1 aspect of Math Workshop across the grades)

INSPIRED BY LIITERACY AT WORK 2022

COACH REFLECTIONS
BOY

COACH: _____
DATE: _____

What do I want to do this year? Why?

What might be some challenges to doing this? How will I address these challenges?

What am I most excited about this year?

What do I want to get better at this year?

What part of Math Workshop do I know really well?

What part of Math Workshop do I want to get better at?

What part of Math Workshop do I need to know more about? How will I find out?

COACH REFLECTIONS
MOY

COACH: _____

DATE: _____

How is the year going overall?

What is going really well?

What is challenging? What can I do about it?

What is the trickiest part of what you do as a Math Coach?

What are 1-3 things I can celebrate this year so far?

What is a big goal for the next part of the year?

COACH REFLECTIONS
EOY

COACH: _____

DATE: _____

How was my year overall?

What went really well?

What do I need to work on for next year?

What was particularly challenging? Why?

Name 1-3 things I can celebrate this year!

What is a big goal for next year?

REFLECTING ON MY COACHING

TEACHER: _____   DATE:_____

COACH:_____   TIME:_____

I make it a point to touch base with all my teachers throughout each quarter.
1 2 3

I have a coaching menu.
1 2 3

I offer a variety of pd throughout the year.
1 2 3

I give quick, actionable feedback.
1 2 3

I celebrate successes.
1 2 3

I read a math article or book every quarter.
1 2 3

I model/demo lessons.
1 2 3

I plan with teachers.
1 2 3

I get along with others.
1 2 3

Teachers trust me.
1 2 3

I encourage risk-taking environments.
1 2 3

I stretch my own pedagogy.
1 2 3

I help teachers set district- and school-aligned math goals.
1 2 3

I encourage teachers to stretch their own pedagogy.
1 2 3

I integrate technology into my pd.
1 2 3

Free Choice.
1 2 3

1 = Yes   2 = Sometimes   3 = Not Yet

Goal Setting with Teachers

 DOI: 10.4324/9781003458975-10

What You will Find in this Section!

In this section you will find forms and documents that help you to set goals with teachers and to set goals for yourself.

Teacher Goals for Math Workshop

TEACHER :_____

GOALS

ACTION PLAN

GOAL COMPLETED

TEACHER GOAL SETTING

TEACHER: _____   DATE:_____
COACH: _____   GRADE:_____

WHAT PART OF MATH WORKSHOP DO YOU WANT TO FOCUS ON?
ENERGIZER/ROUTINES   MATH WORKSTATIONS
MINI-LESSON   CONFERRING
GUIDED MATH   DEBRIEF
                            OTHER _____

Goals

Success Criteria

Action Step 1   Completed ☐

Action Step 2   Completed ☐

Reflection

TEACHER GOAL SETTING

TEACHER: _____   DATE:_____
COACH: _____
GOALS

WHAT PART OF MATH WORKSHOP DO YOU WANT TO GET BETTER AT THIS YEAR?

WHAT IS WORKING REALLY WELL?

HOW CAN I HELP YOU TWEAK A PART OF MATH WORKSHOP?

WHAT CAN I DO TO HELP YOU?

QUOTES

"Our goals can only be reached through a vehicle of a plan, in which we must fervently believe, and upon which we must vigorously act. There is no other route to success."
– Pablo Picasso

What is the state of action planning at your school? Do you all write down the vision and write down the action plan so that you can track the progress towards the vision?

"Setting a goal is not the main thing. It is deciding how you will go about achieving it and staying with that plan."

– Tom Landry

Do all the teachers at your school have goals they are working on? Do they also have action plans? Who do they work with on these goals? What opportunities do they get to reflect and revise their plans? What opportunities do they get to celebrate their successes?

QUOTES

"Unless you have definite, precise, clearly set goals, you are not going to realize the maximum potential that lies within you."

– Zig Ziglar

At your school, do you have school goals, grade goals and individual teacher goals? Does everybody know what these are? How is goal setting promoted even among the students?

Teacher Goals for Math Workshop

TEACHER :_____

GOALS

ACTION PLAN

GOAL COMPLETED

TEACHER GOAL SETTING

TEACHER: _____   DATE:_____

COACH: _____   GRADE:_____

WHAT PART OF MATH WORKSHOP DO YOU WANT TO FOCUS ON?

ENERGIZER/ROUTINES   MATH WORKSTATIONS

MINI-LESSON   CONFERRING

GUIDED MATH   DEBRIEF

                          OTHER _____

Goals

Success Criteria

Action Step 1   Completed ☐

Action Step 2   Completed ☐

Reflection

TEACHER GOAL SETTING

TEACHER: _____   **DATE:** _____

COACH: _____

GOALS

WHAT IS WORKING REALLY WELL?

WHAT PART OF MATH WORKSHOP DO YOU WANT TO GET BETTER AT THIS YEAR?

HOW CAN I HELP YOU TWEAK A PART OF MATH WORKSHOP?

TEACHER GOAL SETTING

TEACHER: _____   COACH: _____

GOAL	
SUCCESS CRITERIA	
ACTION PLAN	COMPLETED ☐
RESOURCES	COMPLETED ☐
COACHING DATES	COMPLETED ☐
DEBRIEF DATES	COMPLETED ☐
NEXT STEPS:	COMPLETED ☐

COACHING SMART GOALS

Teacher:_____   Date: _____

Coach: _____   Time: _____

 **pecific**

- What Exactly do you want to do? Why?

 **easurable**

- What evidence will you collect that proves you have achieved the goal? Is it meaningful?

 **ttainable**

- What are the steps to attain this goal? Is it realistic? Is it action-oriented? Is it agreed upon? What is the alignment with state, district and school goals?

 **elevant**

- How does this goal tie into state, district and school initiatives? Is it results-oriented?

 **imely**

- What is the timeframe to meet this goal? Is it trackable, timely and timebound?

Haughey, D., 2016. S M A R T GOALS. THE ROAD REVIEW, [online] (Fall Issue).
Available at: <https://www.projectsmart.co.uk/smart-goals.php >.

COACHING SMART GOALS

Teacher:_____   Date: _____
Coach: _____   Time: _____

A GOAL SETTING PROTOCOL

Specific — What Exactly do you want to do? Why?

Measurable — What evidence will you collect that proves you have achieved the goal? Is it meaningful?

Attainable — What are the steps to attain this goal? Is it realistic? Is it action-oriented? Is it agreed upon? What is the alignment with state, district and school goals?

Relevant — How does this goal tie into state, district and school initiatives? Is it results-oriented?

Timely — What is the timeframe to meet this goal? Is it trackable, timely and timebound?

Haughey, D., 2016. S M A R T GOALS. THE ROAD REVIEW, [online] (Fall Issue). Available at: <https://www.projectsmart.co.uk/smart-goals.php >.

COACHING SMART GOALS

Teacher: _____   **Date:** _____

Coach: _____   **Time:** _____

A GOAL SETTING PROTOCOL

What exactly do you want to do? Why?

Specific

What evidence will you collect that proves you have achieved the goal? Is it meaningful?

Measurable

Is it attainable, achievable, action-oriented and agreed upon?

Attainable

How does this goal tie into state, district and school initiatives? Is it results-oriented?

Relevant

What is the timeframe to meet this goal? Is it trackable, timely and timebound?

Timely

Haughey, D., 2016. S M A R T GOALS. THE ROAD REVIEW, [online] (Fall Issue).
Available at: <https://www.projectsmart.co.uk/smart-goals.php >.

COACHING SMART GOALS
A TALKING PROTOCOL

Teacher: _____
Coach: _____

Date: _____
Time: _____

S **M** **A** **R** **T**

SPECIFIC	MEASURABLE	ATTAINABLE	RELEVANT	TIMELY
What exactly do you want to do? Why?	What evidence will you collect that proves you have achieved the goal? Is it meaningful?	Is it attainable, achievable, action-oriented and agreed upon?	How does this goal tie into state, district and school initiatives? Is it results-oriented?	What is the time-frame to meet this goal? Is it trackable, timely and time bound?

Haughey, D., 2016. S M A R T GOALS. THE ROAD REVIEW, [online] (Fall Issue). Available at: <https://www.projectsmart.co.uk/smart-goals.php >.

PROBLEM SOLVING PLAN

TEACHER: _____   DATE: _____

WHAT'S THE PROBLEM?

WHY IS IT HAPPENING?

WHAT COULD WE TRY TO DO TO SOLVE IT?

IS THIS WORKING? WHAT ARE THE NEXT STEPS?

Coaching
Data

DOI: 10.4324/9781003458975-11

What You will Find in this Section!

In this section you will find forms and sheets to help guide your conversations around data. You will help teachers to explore the data, look for trends, analyze student work and assessments, interpret the data and come up with next steps for instruction.

COACHING CONVERSATIONS ABOUT ASSESSMENT

Topic: _____
Date: _____
Time: _____
Sign-In
Classroom Visit
Coach
Teacher
Grade

	Glows/Strengths	Grows
What are the multiple ways that data is driving instruction, used to plan math intervention and plan homework		
Diagnostic Assessments		
Formative: Curriculum Quizzes; Progress Monitoring; Ongoing rubrics/Checklists/Math Journals		
Summative: Curriculum Tests; Benchmark Assessments; District Assessments		
What are 2 pieces of Assessment that you want to discuss?		

DATA REVIEW

TEACHER: _____
COACH: _____
GRADE: _____
ASSESSMENT: _____

STRENGTHS	CHALLENGES
What did most students get correct?	What was the problem that many students struggled with?
How did they solve the problem?	What error patterns did they make?
What will you suggest as ongoing practice in workstations and for energizers and routines?	What will you suggest are the next steps? When and where will they re-teach this? How will you check for evidence of learning?

DATA REVIEW

GRADE: _____
ASSESSMENT: _____
TEACHER: _____
COACH: _____

What were the trends in specific classrooms?

What were the trends across the grade?

Which students need the most help?

What will the next instructional steps look like?

DATA REVIEW

GRADE: _____   TEACHER: _____

ASSESSMENT: _____   COACH: _____

STRENGTHS	CHALLENGES
Where did most students demonstrate knowledge?	**What was most challenging for your students?**
How did they solve the problem?	**What error patterns did they make?**
What will you suggest as ongoing practice in workstations and for energizers and routines?	**What will you suggest as the next steps? When and where will you reteach this? How will you check for evidence of learning?**

DATA REVIEW

GRADE: _____   TEACHER: _____

ASSESSMENT: _____   COACH: _____

What were the trends in specific classrooms?

What were the trends across the grade?

Which students need the most help?

Which students have mastered the standard?

What will the next instructional steps look like?

COACHING CONVERSATIONS ABOUT ASSESSMENT

TEACHER: _____   DATE: _____

TIME: _____

	Glows/Strengths	Grows
What are the multiple ways that data is informing intervention and homework?		
Diagnostic Assessments		
Formative: Curriculum Quizzes; Progress Monitoring; Ongoing Rubrics/Checklists/Math Journals		
Summative: Curriculum Tests; Benchmark Assessments; District Assessments		
What are 2 pieces of Assessment that you want to discuss?		

Calendars

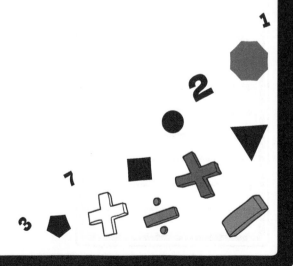

 DOI: 10.4324/9781003458975-12

What You will Find in this Section!

In this section you will find many different types of calendars for planning. There are yearly calendars, quarterly calendars, monthly planners, weekly planners and daily planners.
Planning is the key to success!

YEAR AT GLANCE

JULY	AUGUST
SEPTEMBER	OCTOBER
NOVEMBER	DECEMBER
JANUARY	FEBRUARY

MONTH AT A GLANCE

Goals:
Plans:

June

Goals:
Plans:

July

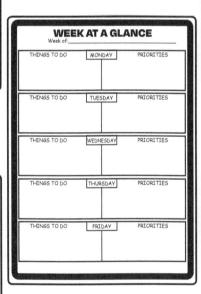

WEEK AT A GLANCE

Week of:_____

THINGS TO DO	MONDAY	PRIORITIES
THINGS TO DO	TUESDAY	PRIORITIES
THINGS TO DO	WEDNESDAY	PRIORITIES
THINGS TO DO	THURSDAY	PRIORITIES
THINGS TO DO	FRIDAY	PRIORITIES

DAILY PLAN

7:00 - 8:00	
8:00 - 9:00	
9:00 - 10:00	
10:00 - 11:00	
11:00 - 12:00	
12:00 - 1:00	
1:00 - 2:00	
2:00 - 3:00	
3:00 - 4:00	
4:00 - 5:00	

QUARTER AT A GLANCE

QUARTER 1	QUARTER 2
QUARTER 3	QUARTER 4

NOTES

QUOTES

"The key is not to prioritize what's on your schedule, but to schedule your priorities."

Stephen Covey.

Prioritizing is the key to success! Have you set out your priorities for the year, month, week and day?

"Failing to plan is planning to fail."

Alan Lakein.

Do you have a plan? Is it written? Have you discussed it with anyone? Who helps you stay accountable to your plans? What do you do to celebrate the successes?

"Don't be busy, be productive."

Tim Ferriss.

Are you busy or productive? How can you prioritize productivity because it is so easy to stay busy?

YEARLY PLANNER

JANUARY

FEBRUARY

MARCH

APRIL

MAY

JUNE

JULY

AUGUST

SEPTEMBER

OCTOBER

NOVEMBER

DECEMBER

Faculty & Staff Birthdays

January	February	March

April	May	June

July	August	September

October	November	December

YEAR AT A GLANCE

JANUARY	FEBRUARY	MARCH

APRIL	MAY	JUNE

YEAR AT A GLANCE

JULY	AUGUST	SEPTEMBER

OCTOBER	NOVEMBER	DECEMBER

YEAR AT A GLANCE

JULY	AUGUST

SEPTEMBER	OCTOBER

NOVEMBER	DECEMBER

JANUARY	FEBRUARY

YEAR AT A GLANCE

MARCH	APRIL

MAY	JUNE

NOTES

QUARTER AT A GLANCE

QUARTER 1	QUARTER 2

QUARTER 3	QUARTER 4

NOTES

Month at a Glance
August

Goals:

Plans:

September

Goals:

Plans:

Month at a Glance
October

Goals:

Plans:

November

Goals:

Plans:

Month at a Glance
December

Goals:

Plans:

January

Goals:

Plans:

Month at a Glance
February

Goals:

Plans:

March

Goals:

Plans:

Month at a Glance
April

Goals:

Plans:

May

Goals:

Plans:

Month at a Glance
June

Goals:

Plans:

July

Goals:

Plans:

WEEKLY PLAN

☐ **MONDAY**

☐ **TUESDAY**

☐ **WEDNESDAY**

☐ **THURSDAY**

☐ **FRIDAY**

☐ **TO-DO**

Week at a Glance

Week of:_____

MONDAY

TUESDAY

WEDNESDAY

THURSDAY

FRIDAY

Week at a Glance

Week of:_____

THINGS TO DO	MONDAY	PRIORITIES

THINGS TO DO	TUESDAY	PRIORITIES

THINGS TO DO	WEDNESDAY	PRIORITIES

THINGS TO DO	THURSDAY	PRIORITIES

THINGS TO DO	FRIDAY	PRIORITIES

Day at a Glance

Date :_____

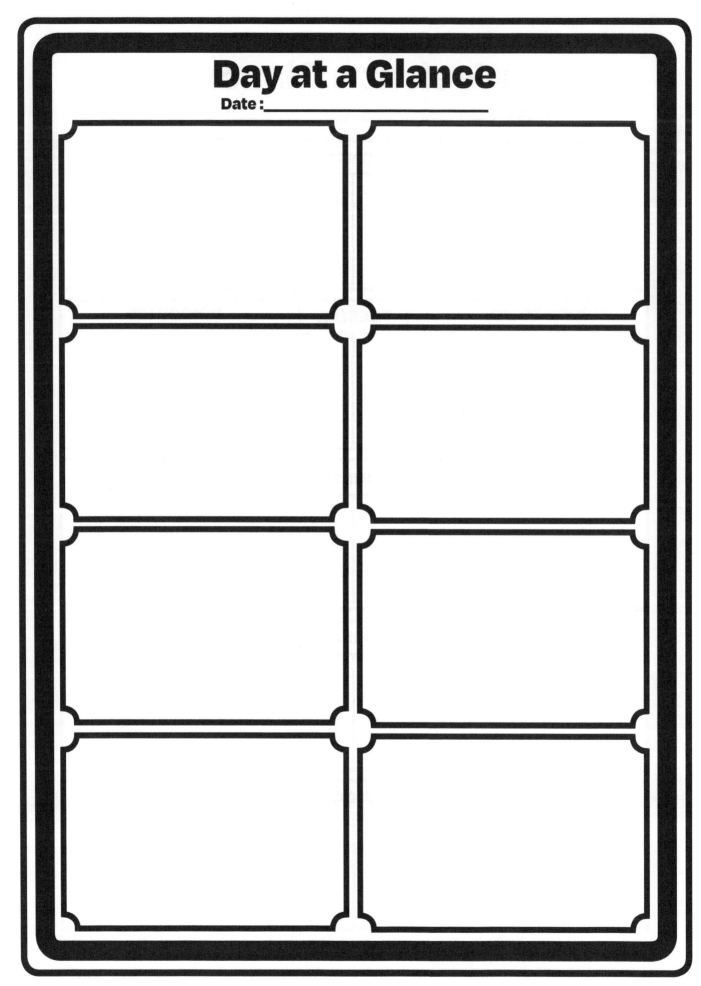

Day at a Glance

Date :_____

7:00 – 8:00	**12:00 – 1:00**
8:00 – 9:00	**1:00 – 2:00**
9:00 – 10:00	**2:00 – 3:00**
10:00 – 11:00	**3:00 – 4:00**
11:00 – 12:00	**4:00 – 5:00**

Day at a Glance

Date :_____

7:00 - 8:00	**11:00 - 12:00**
8:00 - 9:00	**12:00 - 1:00**
9:00 - 10:00	**1:00 - 2:00**
10:00 - 11:00	**2:00 - 3:00**

Day at a Glance

Date :_____

7:00 - 8:00

8:00 -9:00

9:00 - 10:00

10:00 - 11:00

11:00 - 12:00

Day at a Glance

Date :_____

12:00 - 1:00

1:00 -2:00

2:00 - 3:00

3:00 - 4:00

Day at a Glance

Date :_____

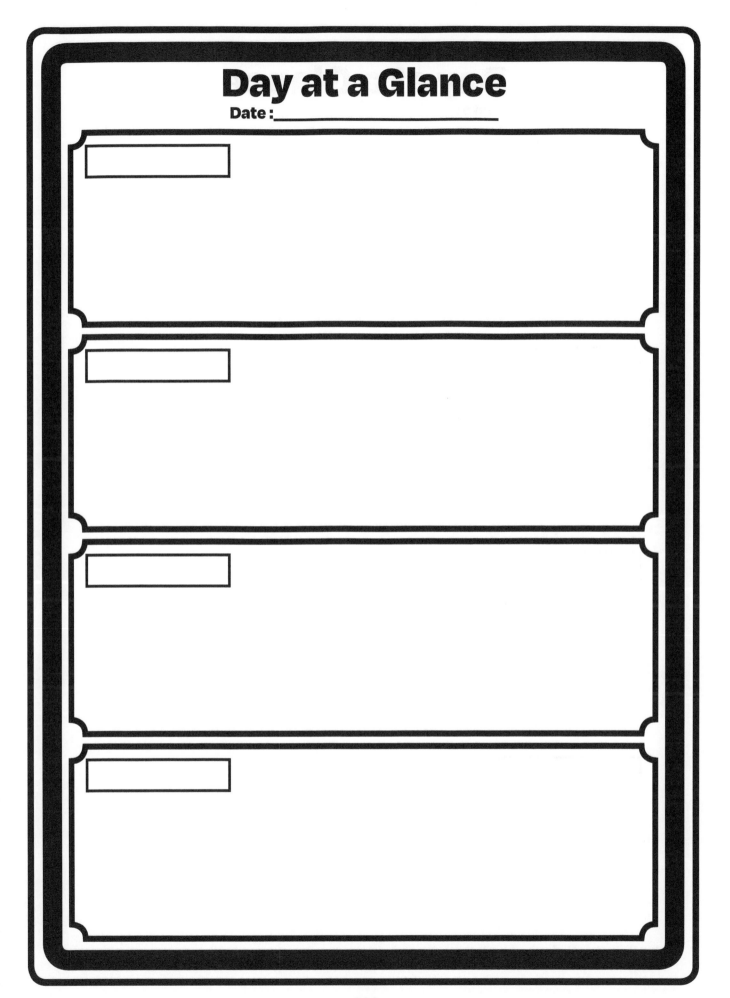

Day at a Glance

Date :_____

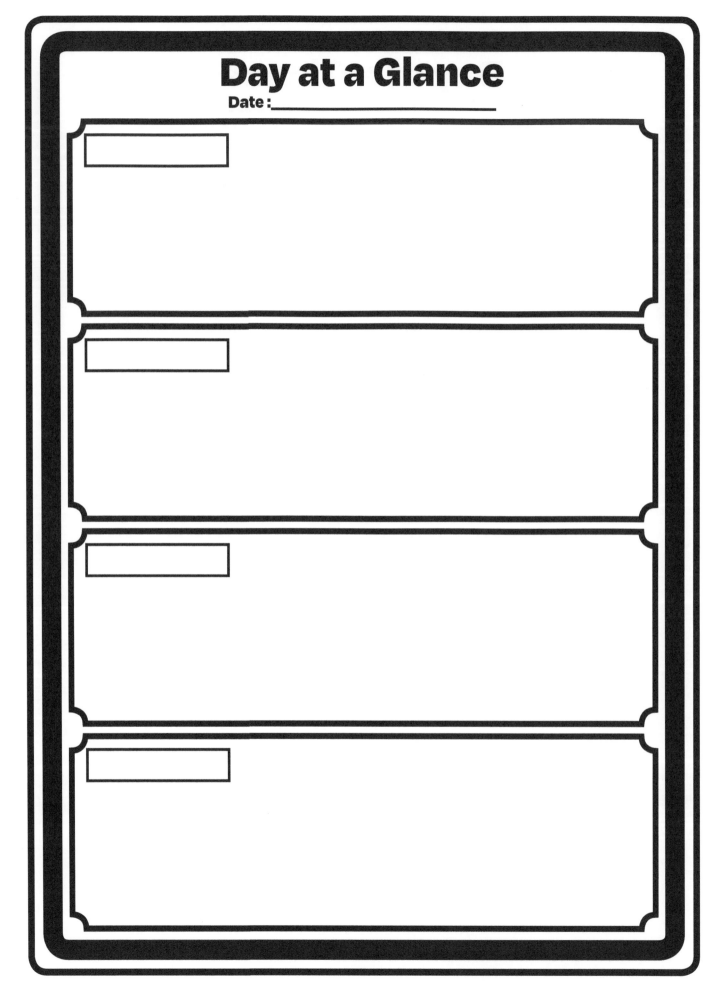

Day at a Glance

Date :_____

THINGS TO DO		PRIORITIES

THINGS TO DO		PRIORITIES

THINGS TO DO		PRIORITIES

THINGS TO DO		PRIORITIES

Day at a Glance

Date :_____

THINGS TO DO · PRIORITIES

THINGS TO DO · PRIORITIES

THINGS TO DO · PRIORITIES

THINGS TO DO · PRIORITIES

Day at a Glance

Date :_____

Grade Level :_____   Time :_____

Subject :_____   Unit :_____

DAY	ACTIVITY	COMPLETED/NEXT STEPS

DAILY PLAN

7:00 - 8:00

8:00 - 9:00

9:00 - 10:00

10:00 - 11:00

11:00 - 12:00

12:00 - 1:00

1:00 - 2:00

2:00 - 3:00

3:00 - 4:00

4:00 - 5:00

To Do Lists

 DOI: 10.4324/9781003458975-13

What You will Find in this Section!

In this section you will find templates that help you to do those quick to do lists. Lists are another way to stay organized. The fun part is being able to check the completed box!

To Do List

To do today	To do this week

To do this month	To do this year

TO DO LIST

Things to do	Done

TO DO LIST

Thing to do	Started	Finished

TO DO LIST

Thing to do	Started	Finished

TO DO LIST

Things to do	Done

To Do List

To do today

To do this week

To do this month

To do this year

Materials
Log

DOI: 10.4324/9781003458975-14

What You will Find in this Section!

In this section you will find templates to help keep track of all the materials that you will hand out, loan out and buy this year.

TEACHER MATERIALS CHECKED OUT

Math Resource	Teacher	Check Out Date	Returned Date

TEACHER MATERIALS CHECKED OUT

Math Resource	Teacher	Check Out Date	Returned Date

Things to Buy

DOI: 10.4324/9781003458975-15

THINGS TO BUY

What	When	Why	Vendor	Cost	Ordered	Received

Book Study Planning Sheets

 DOI: 10.4324/9781003458975-16

BOOK STUDY PLAN

BOOK:

WHY WE CHOSE THIS BOOK:

DATE	CHAPTERS	DISCUSSION QUESTIONS	ACTION ITEMS

REFERENCES

Connecticut Department of Education: Making the most out of Coaching retrieved https://portal.ct.gov > Math > Math-Coaching-final

Fitzpatrick, S. (2022) How to be an effective Math Coach: Five Key Strategies. Retrieved on March 3 from https://www.hmhco.com/blog/how-to-be-an-effective-math-coach

Making the Most Out of Math Coaches - CT.gov https://portal.ct.gov > Math > Math-Coaching-final

About Dr. Nicki

Dr. Nicki Newton is an education consultant who works with schools and districts around the country and Canada on k-8 math curriculum. She has taught elementary school, middle school, and graduate school. Dr Nicki has an Ed.M. and an Ed.D from Teachers College, Columbia University. She is greatly interested in teaching and learning practices around the world and has researched education in Denmark, Guatemala and India. She has written several books, including *Guided Math*, *Math Workshop* and *Math Running Records*. She is currently a part of the curriculum team for the new McGraw Hill Reveal Math series. Her latest book is called *Accelerating Math in K-8 Classrooms*. She is presently writing and researching a book about high dosage tutoring. She enjoys visiting schools and working with adminstrators, teachers and students in their classrooms face-to-face and virtually.

CONTACT US!

guidedmath123 & math running records

drnickimath

guidedmathinaction

https://www.pinterest.com/drnicki7/

drnickinewton

www.drnickinewton.com

HAPPY MATHING!

For Product Safety Concerns and Information please contact our
EU representative GPSR@taylorandfrancis.com Taylor & Francis
Verlag GmbH, Kaufingerstraße 24, 80331 München, Germany